More Praise for "The Road To Retirement 2.0"

"Jeff's book provides expecting retirees a clear overview of investment principals and key tools for preparing to reasonably evaluate, plan for and generate income from one's retirement accounts. It's important advice for anyone in this situation."

— *Karina M. Thomas of Schafer Thomas Maez PC*

"I have always looked for professionals to help me navigate new areas of my life. If I have an automobile issue, I seek out a good auto mechanic. There is no way that you can be an expert in ever important subject in your life. I help people with Medicare decisions. It's a complicated subject and important to get advice from a trusted source. Retirement planning is even more complex than Medicare. I'm glad to have Jeff's knowledge to help steer the way. The more you put off planning for retirement, the more it's probably going to cost you in the long-run. Jeff Townsend is like a trusted friend, confidant and advisor. His experience and wealth of knowledge comes through on every page of this short, powerful book."

— *Liz Tredennick, Medicare Insurance Agent*

"The last thing most people want to deal with is planning for retirement or even thinking about retirement—until it's too late. And for those people, **The Road to Retirement** is a terrific book. It's an easy, fast read, broken into logical, informative bite-sized chapters, and It covers everything you need to know now about retirement. I highly recommend it."

—Randy L. Kite, CPA
Ian D. Gardenswartz & Associates, P.C

"With straight talk, Jeff Townsend helps readers navigate the overwhelming number of financial products and services in today's rapidly changing markets. Townsend has always believed in rigorous, rational financial planning — not emotional decision making, timing the markets, playing hunches, buying into rumors, tinkering with portfolios, or chasing tips from friends. His five-step investment process provides a framework for identifying, analyzing and executing investment opportunities. **The Road to Retirement** is a guide that speaks to serious investors about the most serious of subjects: a safe, sound retirement."

—Cindy Munro, Liberty Bookkeeping Services LLC

THE ROAD TO
RETIREMENT
2.0

The Road To Retirement 2.0
Everything You Need to Know for a Successful Retirement
Copyright © 2018 Jeffery E. Townsend

Book design by:
Arbor Services, Inc.
www.arborservices.co/

Printed in the United States of America

The Road To Retirement 2.0
Everything You Need to Know for a Successful Retirement
Jeffery E. Townsend

1. Title 2. Author 3. Retirement Planning

Library of Congress Control Number: 2017909190
ISBN 13: 978-0-692-88474-4

THE ROAD TO RETIREMENT

2.0

Jeffery E. Townsend

This book is dedicated to
the brave military members who have put service before self and
have offered unquestionable sacrifices in defense of this nation

Contents

Acknowledgments

I'd like to give special thanks to all the brave men and women who serve in our armed forces and protect our freedoms, which all too often we take for granted. If not for our soldiers, our country—and thus our free markets—wouldn't be what they are today.

I have had a fabulous career of over thirty years, which was made possible only with the patience and support of my wonderful wife, Cayle.

My beautiful daughters, Nellie and Emma, continue to remind me what's important in life.

This book wouldn't have been possible if not for the continued trust and confidence of our great clients. I'd also like to give thanks for our talented staff that have helped make our firm one of the leading independent retirement planning firms in the country. They have done this by providing our clients a first-class retirement experience, which will become the platinum standard for our industry.

Introduction:

The Importance of Retirement Planning

Today's retirees face many complex challenges that, for all intents and purposes, didn't exist fifty, twenty-five, or in some cases, even ten years ago. Securing retirement income in a dynamic but often volatile economy that faces severe fiscal and social issues can at best seem like a risky proposition, and at worst like navigating through an unswept minefield left over from wars past.

A case in point is the state of corporate pensions. Due to recent economic and political trends, retirees must understand the risks to their hard-earned pensions and take the appropriate steps to mitigate those risks. And of course, skyrocketing health care costs can put enormous pressure on even financially comfortable families.

One of the main reasons for the increased volatility in our economy is the impending exodus of the baby boomers from the workforce.

While this issue is getting much attention, I've heard hundreds of different scenarios that run the gamut from doomsday to a new golden age. What is clear, though, is that American baby boomers are turning sixty-five at the rate of more than ten thousand every day throughout the USA. That's almost seven people every minute. As Bloomberg reported in January 2017, in the fourth quarter of 2016 the number of Americans aged sixty-five or older without a disability who were not in the labor force rose by 800,000. Despite some boomers continuing to work longer than their parents did, millions more are headed for retirement.

When they retire, people begin withdrawing money from their retirement and investment accounts instead of contributing to them. Most will begin drawing Social Security benefits and other entitlements. All, however, will leave the full-time workforce and cease paying into the Social Security trust fund, creating for the first time in our history a negative ratio of workers to retirees. Predicting how this phenomenon will impact our economy and making the necessary adjustments will be the most important and challenging task that our leaders will ever undertake.

In the decades ahead, Social Security, Medicare, Medicaid, and other entitlement programs are likely to look quite different. Health care costs will likely continue to rise, and in order to pay these costs, insurers will cut back on the procedures they cover. And politicians will likely continue to dance around these issues.

Taken together, these conditions comprise a cold front bringing nasty weather our direction. But with proper planning, the bad weather can remain outside the house, while inside is safe and warm.

We Americans like to see ourselves as a self-sufficient people. Therefore, every American whose financial situation is dependent upon the health of our economy must make a solid set of retirement plans, because the retirement parachute that past generations have counted on may not be there for current and future generations.

As a retirement advisor, I find that when folks reach the age of fifty, they begin to think about retirement. The nagging question of whether or not they'll be able to afford retirement weighs upon their minds and hearts.

Before long, all seventy-six million of us baby boomers will be reaching retirement age. But not everyone will find gold in their golden years. Not all of the folks with whom I meet are sufficiently capitalized for the comfortable retirement they envision. By "sufficiently capitalized," I mean having enough money both for their preretirement lifestyle and enough to provide for them after retirement and for the rest of their lives.

Because of poor decisions and failing to seek out advice, many hardworking Americans have seen their hopes for a dream retirement evaporate, along with their retirement savings. Others have seen their incomes shrink because companies have decided to terminate their pensions.

Some have simply avoided thinking about getting older altogether. After all, none of us likes to admit that that's what's happening to us. It's not only an acknowledgment that we're mortal, but also that we're approaching the same end that other mortals have come to since the beginning of time.

Admittedly, we prefer to think about pleasant things. In 2014 a *CNN Money* article reported that people surveyed spent an average of five hours planning their next vacation. Retirement planning? About forty-five minutes per year.

Are You Prepared?

45 MINUTES

12 HOURS

Source: *USA Today*, March 12, 1996

And then there are those who do manage to think about retirement from time to time, but fail to actively plan for it. Generally, these people assume that whatever pieces of the retirement puzzle are already in place—their pension, Social Security, and personal savings—will be sufficient. They never actually take the time to sit down and run the numbers. If they did, chances are they would realize that eventually they're going to be behind the eight ball. In fact, it's my opinion that the number one reason most people fail in retirement is from lack of planning. The old saying is true: People don't plan to fail; they fail to plan.

I'll admit it's not always easy. The ranges of tasks that fall under retirement planning are broad and can be quite complicated. From investments and taxes to insurance and estate planning, these issues can be daunting and even overwhelming.

When Social Security was created in 1935, the average life expectancy was sixty-five. There wasn't much to look forward to after you retired, especially since the Social Security Administration decided the normal retirement age was the same as the average age at death—sixty-five. Most of us still think of age sixty-five as a normal retirement age. The only difference is that we are living considerably longer. In fact, thanks to modem medicine, those who live into their sixties have a 37% chance of living into their nineties, according to a *U.S. News* article entitled "Life after Age 90."

Living longer sounds great, doesn't it? Or at least it may, until you realize it means your money needs to last twenty-five years or more. Even if you seem to have enough money, what if you or your spouse has health issues? Or what if you experience runaway inflation or a prolonged bear market? There is so much to think about. As one client said to me, "Growing older is not for wimps."

In his book *Age Power*, gerontologist and author Ken Dychtwald reports that one-third of boomers are prepared for retirement, one-third will have to work until about seventy to maintain their current standard of living in retirement, and one third are heading toward poverty in retirement because they are so completely unprepared.

It's true that some people begin to plan for their retirement as soon as they start working, but they're the exception; most wait until they're in their fifties. Some may feel that planning and saving will get easier once the kids leave the nest, or perhaps when they're earning more. Unfortunately, by waiting, the money you save will have fewer years to compound.

Here's an example.

The Early Bird Gets the Bigger Worm

Bob and Mary are both thirty years old and plan to retire in thirty-five years. Mary begins to save $2,000 annually for ten years to an account that earns 10%, and then discontinues any further contributions. Bob, on the other hand, waits ten years before starting his retirement savings, at which point he begins to deposit $2,000 annually into an account that also earns 10 percent. Bob contributes into his account for twenty-five years. Who do you suppose comes out ahead?

Thanks to compound interest, by the time Mary reaches age sixtyfive, her contribution of $20,000 during the first ten years will have reached an account balance of about $418,000. Bob, on the other hand, while contributing $50,000, will have a balance of only about $240,000 at age sixty-five. Pretty incredible, isn't it? As Albert Einstein once said, "Compound interest is the most powerful force in the universe."

Retirement planning is no longer a luxury reserved only for the wealthy. Rather, it is a necessity for anyone who wants to increase their chances for a successful retirement. Consider the following issues:

- Most employer retirement plans typically do not replace 100% of one's preretirement salary. In fact, many employers' plans only replace about a third—and that's assuming they provide a pension at all.

- Many retirees will have to deal with poor health, which will mean increased medical expenses for services, medicine, and equipment. Such expenses can quickly deplete even the healthiest of retirement savings.
- Cost of living doesn't necessarily go down just because you're retired. Even though your house payment *may* be gone (most retirees do not have their homes paid for) and your car may be paid off, you may have plenty of other expenses, such as travel, medical bills, home repairs, entertainment, clothing, groceries, and future car purchases.
- Social Security alone will, at best, only cover minimum needs. Social Security was never intended to cover everything; it was meant to be a supplement.
- In fact, the more you made while working, the less Social Security you will get as a percentage of income.
- Inflation is here to stay! Just because you're retired doesn't mean that inflation retires. Even with a modest 3% inflation rate, your income will need to double over thirty years just to keep even. And with life expectancies increasing, living twenty-five to thirty years after retirement is a real possibility.

Thinking Short Term?

What will it cost to maintain a $30,000 per year Standard of Living with 3% inflation?

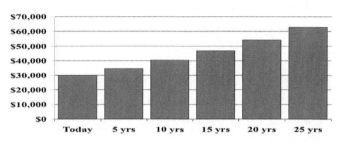

Be prepared to double your money if you're retired for 25 years.

The very purpose of retirement planning is to identify your goals and objectives, and to develop strategies to meet them. In order to develop a meaningful retirement plan you will need to figure out how much capital you have now that can be used for future retirement income, how much capital you'll need in the future, and how you get from where you are today to where you want to be tomorrow.

In addition to wealth accumulation are many other considerations, such as risk management. You must determine what your retirement picture might look like in the event of a death or disability. Might such an event cause early depletion of your retirement nest egg?

Excessive liability will require more capital just to cover the debt service. We live in a time when "buy now, pay later" is the norm. I believe you will find that it's much easier to pay off debt than it is to accumulate enough capital to service that debt.

Changes in employment can alter your plans. Corporate downsizing and the general willingness to change jobs for a better one have increased over the years, and may make it difficult to be vested in any employer plans. Terminated employees are also likely to have to spend some of the money they intended for retirement, and may have to deal with a lump-sum rollover for any vested interest in an employer plan.

Taxes can make it difficult to save for retirement. Let's face it, the more we can save in taxes, the more we may have to save for retirement or spend in retirement. Our tax code is one of the most complicated in the world. Since taxes are typically one of our largest expenses, becoming a little more knowledgeable in this area can be quite beneficial.

And finally, two of the most overlooked areas of retirement planning are having the proper planning in place to take care of you in the event you become incapacitated or incompetent, and planning for the distribution of your estate after death. Here again, the dread and anxiety that accompanies thinking about such things keeps many people from addressing these important issues.

In the following chapters I'll discuss these issues and many more. Information is the cornerstone upon which every successful retirement plan is built. Knowing yourself and your options is the first step toward building a comprehensive retirement plan that will serve you and your family for the rest of your life and beyond.

Chapter One:

Testing Your Financial Knowledge

Do you know enough to plan your retirement? The concept seems simple enough: Set aside a little money each year and don't touch it until you retire. Add in the income you'll get from Social Security and any employer pension plans (assuming they're still around), and you've got your retirement income. However, *understanding* this concept and knowing how to *make it work for you* are two different issues.

One of the main problems is that the various elements involved in putting together a successful plan are ever changing, so much so that the best financial planning professionals continue their education to keep up with the changes and maintain their professional designations. From percentages and contribution limits to rates and penalties, a whole host of variables can change at the whim of Congress or the

Federal Reserve. Moreover, with the economy in such a volatile state of flux, you need to plan carefully.

That said, the decision to begin planning for your retirement is probably the single most important and best financial decision you will ever make. Whether you're in your twenties or your fifties or even sixties, it's never too early or late. Granted, the earlier you start, the longer you have for your money to work for you. But even later in life, you can enact a strategy that will drastically improve your financial outlook during retirement.

The key is to actually *do it*.

One reason many people put off retirement planning is because they are unsure of where to start. They know they have Social Security coming at some point, and possibly a pension from their current job. Beyond that, they don't have much of anything else set up or, for that matter, even know what's available. They've heard about IRAs and such, and that there may be certain things they can do in terms of taxes. But they don't truly understand what's involved.

One of the things I've found to be helpful to clients is a short quiz that helps them understand the issues in play and gives them an idea of what's out there for them. It's a tough quiz, and don't be surprised if many of the questions stump you! But have fun, and when you're done you'll find the answers at the end.

Retirement Quiz

1. Under current law, if you retire today, the earliest you can start taking retirement Social Security distribution is:

A) 65

B) 62

C) 68

D) 70

2. With traditional tax-deductible IRAs, you must begin taking distributions by what age?

A) 65 1/2

B) 68

C) 75

D) 70 1/2

3. With a Roth IRA, the latest age by which you have to take distributions is:

A) 70 1/2

B) 75

C) 65

D) Never

4. One of the differences between a Roth IRA and a traditional IRA is:

A) With a traditional IRA, you can deduct your IRA contribution the year you make it, and you can't with a Roth.

B) You can deduct your Roth contribution the year you make it, but you can't with your traditional contribution.

C) The tax-deductible IRA contribution is a credit against your taxes, so if you contribute $2,000 you pay $2,000 less in taxes.

D) There is no difference between the two.

5. The difference between a Roth IRA and a traditional IRA during the accumulation period is that during the period *after* you put your money in and *before* you take it out:

A) You get taxed on your Roth earnings every year, but not for your traditional IRA earnings.

B) You get taxed on the traditional IRA but not on the Roth.

C) With a traditional IRA, if you have a loss you can claim it that year, which you can't do with a Roth.

D) There isn't any; you don't pay taxes on either plan.

6. Internal Revenue Code Section 72(t) covers:

A) Distributions from qualified plans after age 70

B) Distributions from 457 plans

C) Distributions from 403(b) plans

D) Distributions prior to age 59 ½

7. Sam, age fifty-seven, opts to take an early distribution from his retirement plan, using the IRC 72(t) distribution method.

At what age could he make a change to the payment stream without incurring a penalty?

A) He can't change the payment stream at any point without penalty.

B) 59 1/2

C) 60

D) 62

8. Required distributions are taxed at what rate?

A) The participant's ordinary income tax rate

B) Capital gains tax rate

C) 20%

D) 10%

9. At what point must a participant in a 403(b) plan begin minimum distributions?

A) When the participant reaches the age of 59.

B) When the participant reaches the age of 65.

C) When the participant reaches the age of 70.

D) When the participant reaches the age of 70 1/2.

10. What is the consequence of making an IRA contribution that is more than the allowable amount?

A) The excess is subject to a penalty tax.

B) The account loses its tax-advantaged status.

C) Future contributions are prohibited.

D) The entire account balance must be distributed no later than December 31 of the year in which the excess contribution was made.

11. Bob was born August 1, 1931. What is Bob's required beginning date for purposes of the minimum distribution rules?

A) August 1, 2001
B) December 31, 2001
C) April 15, 2002
D) April 1, 2003

12. All of the following are designed to provide for discretionary distributions EXCEPT:

A) Traditional IRA plans
B) Roth IRA plans
C) SEP plans
D) Pension plans

13. In 1999, Eileen, age fifty-seven, opened a Roth IRA with a $2,000 contribution. Over the next three years she made additional contributions totaling $4,500. Now, at the end of the fourth year, her account is valued at $8,000, with $6,500 in contributions and $1,500 in earnings. She then withdraws $7,000. Which of the following statements is CORRECT?

A) The $7,000 withdrawal is not subject to income tax or penalty.

B) Of the $7,000 withdrawal, $500 is subject to income tax.

C) Of the $7,000 withdrawal, $6,500 is subject to income tax.

D) Of the $7,000 withdrawal, $500 is subject to income tax and penalty.

14. If Randy's required minimum distribution from his profit-sharing plan is $7,500 and he takes $5,000, the penalty would be:

A) $1,250

B) $2,500

C) $3,750

D) $5,000

15. The penalty for taking more than the required distribution in any given year is:

A) Zero percent

B) 10%

C) 20%

D) 50%

16. Which of the following factors could preclude an individual from contributing to a traditional IRA?

A) Age

B) Participation in a qualified employer plan

C) Level of adjusted gross income

D) Income tax filing status

17. In order to have retirement benefits based on your ex-spouse's Social Security earnings, you must have been married:

A) Five years

B) Twenty years

C) Ten years

D) There is no time requirement as long as you were legally married.

18. If, when you retire, you choose an annuity instead of a lump sum payment, and you choose a joint and survivor annuity, which of the following is true?

A) When you and your spouse die, even if it's only three months after you start receiving payments, your heirs get nothing.

B) Monthly payments stop when you die, so your spouse gets nothing.

C) You are guaranteed monthly payments for ten years, and if you die during that time your beneficiary will get income for the rest of the ten-year period.

D) If you die before your spouse, he or she continues to receive the same amount of money as if you were alive.

19. An IRA owner dies at the age of sixty-one. His daughter, age thirty-eight, is the beneficiary. The daughter elects to take 100% of the IRA immediately. What is the tax and penalty situation on this distribution?

A) Daughter pays income taxes; there is no penalty.

B) Daughter pays income taxes and a 10% penalty.

C) Dad's estate pays income taxes; there is no penalty.

D) Dad's estate pays income taxes and a 10% penalty.

20. All of the following could be rolled over to their own IRA except:

A) Jean, age forty-nine, an ex-spouse who received a portion of her husband's profit-sharing plan under the terms of a QDRO

B) Paul, age sixty-seven, who retired under the terms of his plan's early retirement provision and received a lump-sum distribution from his 401(k) plan

C) Mary, age sixty-eight, the beneficiary of her deceased husband's traditional IRA; minimum distributions had already begun on a discretionary basis

D) Carl, age forty-four, the beneficiary under his deceased sister's defined benefit plan; the sister died at the age of fifty-four

Answers: 1-B, 2-D, 3-D, 4-A, 5-D, 6-D, 7-D, 8-A, 9-D, 10-A, 11-D, 12-D, 13-B, 14-A, 15-A, 16-A, 17-C, 18-A, 19-A, 20-D.

How did you do? If you got seventeen or more correct, you have a good handle on the complex issues of retirement. Regardless of your score, I believe you'll benefit greatly from the chapters that lie ahead. Knowledge is the most powerful tool you'll have while you're developing a successful retirement strategy.

Chapter Two:

Projecting Retirement Income Needs and Sources

So now you're ready to get started. You know how much you don't know and how much you do know. You have an idea of the issues you need to address, as well as some of the tools and options available to you.

The first thing you'll want to do is to project your income needs and sources.

Projecting retirement income needs is about as tricky as projecting what you're likely to be hungry for ten, twenty, or even thirty years from now. To make matters worse, politicians are constantly enacting new policies that can have profound effects on what retirees can expect in their golden years.

Medicare and Social Security are under pressure, and if not overhauled, it's a virtual certainty that the amount of benefits you'll receive will be decreased while the number of retirees is about to drastically increase. The age when benefits kick in is likely to be pushed back as well.

In this chapter, I'll discuss the basics of projecting your income needs during retirement, and then examine the most common sources of income for most people in their later years: Social Security, employee pensions (including "do-it yourself" pensions), and personal savings and investments.

First Things First: How Much Do You Need?

One of the biggest mistakes people make is drastically underestimating how much income they'll need during their retirement. While it is true that some expenses will have decreased by retirement, such as transportation, dependent care, and food and clothing costs for work, other expenses will increase, including property taxes, repairs and maintenance, recreation costs, and perhaps most significantly, medical expenses.

I have found that at the end of the day, most people want to maintain their preretirement lifestyle. This means maintaining a robust level of income, based on their needs and wants. The most obvious way to determine income needs is to analyze current budgets and spending patterns. Generally, overall expenses during retirement tend to be 70 to 80% of preretirement expenses. However, it's always best to overestimate and be safe. Because many retirees want to maintain their preretirement lifestyle, it may be more appropriate to budget the full amount of their current income and expenses. Granted, some costs will decrease or stop altogether, but others that do not currently figure in may appear, such as health care costs.

Another factor to figure in is inflation. Even at low levels, it drastically affects purchasing power over time.

For instance, if you decide you need $60,000 of retirement income annually to maintain your current standard of living at age sixty-five, with 3% inflation, by the time you're seventy your income will have to increase to nearly $70,000; by the time you're eighty, to maintain your current standard of living your income would have to be nearly $94,000. Or, if you're younger when establishing income needs for retirement, say age forty-five, by the time you're ready to retire in twenty years, you would need over $108,000 to maintain the standard of living that $60,000 gives you now. Software programs are available to help determine amounts of income needed to compensate for inflation.

While income sources like Social Security and Medicare benefits are indexed to reflect inflation, most pension benefits are not. Obviously, knowing which sources of income are subject to inflation and which aren't is important. A good inflation evaluation by a qualified retirement planner can be invaluable.

It's also a good idea to do periodic analyses of your situation to make sure you're on track. Economic factors, such as inflation and new tax laws, are likely to change during the lead-up to retirement.

Where Will the Money Come From?

If you're like most people, you have a vague idea that some of your retirement income will come from Social Security, some may come from a pension plan, and some may come from a few small investments—a little from this and a little from that, basically. To most people, it's as much a mystery as the ingredients in sausage.

There are primarily three main sources of retirement income:

1. Social Security
2. Employer-sponsored retirement plans
3. Personal savings and investments

I'll discuss each of these in the following pages. I'll also briefly discuss Supplementary Security Income (SSI), which is a program run by the Social Security Administration that supplements the Social Security benefits of poorer Americans.

Social Security

Virtually every employed or self-employed person is covered by Social Security. While Social Security benefits are an important source of retirement income, they are not adequate to support a comfortable retirement for most people. For instance, if in 2017 your household income was the median of $62,802 (as the US Census Bureau reported for peoples aged fifty-five to sixty-four), you can expect to receive benefits equal to about 40% of preretirement income. Higher earners can expect far less. As the Social Security website says, "Social Security benefits are typically computed using 'average indexed monthly earnings' (AIME). This average summarizes up to 35 years of a worker's indexed earnings. We apply a formula to this average to compute the primary insurance amount (PIA). The PIA is the basis for the benefits that are paid to an individual."

Here's an example of how the Social Security Administration computes payments, as explained on the website:

"For example, a person who had maximum-taxable earnings in each year since age 22, and who retires at age 62 in 2017, would have an average indexed monthly earnings (AIME) equal to $9,784. Based on this AIME amount and the bend points $885 and $5,336, the primary insurance amounts (PIA) would equal $2,888.00. This person would receive a reduced benefit based on the $2,888.00 PIA. The first cost-of-living adjustment (COLA) this individual could receive is the one effective for December 2017."

As I mentioned in the previous chapter, Social Security will be going through changes in the coming years, one way or the other. If it remains essentially the same type of system that it has been since the Great Depression, benefits will undoubtedly decrease and the age at which benefits may be collected will be pushed back. If a fundamental change in how it is funded occurs, for instance, one involving the stock market, it will be increasingly difficult to project the value of benefits paid out, and benefits will likely decrease and the age at which they may be collected will be pushed back.

All this will come as a shock to those who think that Social Security benefits are the only source of income they'll need when they retire. These benefits are not now, nor were they when the program was established in 1935, intended to fully replace their earnings. And if current trends and patterns hold, the dollar value of benefits relative to the cost of living in our increasingly expensive culture will decrease.

That's why it's so important to plan to supplement Social Security benefits with pensions, savings, investments, and other income.

You can, however—at least under the current system, which is based upon current workers paying for current retirees—estimate the amount you'll be receiving from Social Security. How? It's actually quite simple to estimate the monthly benefit amount you'll be entitled to. If you're over sixty, call your local Social Security office and ask for it, or you can also use the online estimator: https://www.ssa.gov/oact/quickcalc/. If you're under sixty, ask the office for a Request for Earnings and Benefit Estimate Statement. Since the more information you have when planning your retirement, the more likely you are to be successful, this statement can be invaluable.

You can also go online and use the Online Calculator. Just Google "Social Security calculator," and it will appear at the top of the results page.

Key Questions Retirees Ask

Following are some of the questions retirees ask most often.

When and how do I apply for benefits?
You should apply for Social Security benefits at least three months before you retire. It's your responsibility to initiate the process—the government will not automatically start sending you checks.

What documents do I need to apply?
✓ Social Security card

✓ Birth certificate or other proof of age

✓ Evidence of recent earnings (i.e., your last W-2, or a copy of your self-employment tax return)

✓ Proof of your spouse's or ex-spouse's death if you are applying for survivors' benefits

At what age can I begin to receive retirement benefits?

You can begin receiving money at age sixty-two, but not full benefits. Under current policies, most people qualify for full benefits between the ages of sixty-five and sixty-seven. The early and late retirement options affect the amount of benefits you receive. Those who retire at sixty-two will have their benefits reduced by about 20% because they will be receiving an additional thirty-six payments.

Beginning in 2000, the age at which full benefits are payable has gradually increased from sixty-five, and in 2022 will reach sixty-seven. Reduced benefits will still be available at age sixty-two, but the reduction will also be larger. Keep in mind, however, that perhaps profound changes are in store for the Social Security system. It's almost a certainty that the age at which benefits kick in will be pushed back to help pay for the increasing number of retirees and dwindling number of workers paying into the system.

Will a return to work affect the amount I receive in benefits?

If you return to work after you start receiving benefits, you will lose $1 for every $2 you earn above the annual exemption amount if you're under full retirement age. Here again, changes to the system will likely affect benefit limits. Since the year 2000, the age at which the earnings test applies has gradually increased as the retirement age rises. Keep in mind that you can stop receiving Social Security benefits if it looks like you might exceed the annual exemption. You can restart your benefits later.

Are my benefits taxable?

If one-half your benefits *plus all your non–Social Security income* exceed a base amount, up to 85% of your benefits may then be subject to federal income tax. The base amount changes each year, so check with your local Social Security office or a CPA for the current amount and specific stipulations.

What about survivor benefits?

If you are widowed, you may qualify for Social Security survivor benefits based on the earnings record of your deceased spouse. Even if you are divorced you may qualify for benefits, provided the marriage lasted at least ten years. Call your local Social Security office for details.

Supplemental Security Income (SSI)

According to a survey sponsored by the American Association of Retired Persons (AARP), almost half of the older persons eligible for Supplementary Security Income (SSI) do not receive benefits because they are unaware of the program or do not know how to apply. SSI is an income-support program run by the Social Security Administration that provides monthly cash payments to low-income adults over sixty-five or to people of any age who are blind or disabled.

This income support is above and beyond what you may already be receiving. Check with your Social Security office for eligibility requirements, as they vary from state to state.

Pensions

Employer-sponsored retirement plans are another important source of retirement income for many people. And as with Social Security, people don't always know what's in store for them in terms of their particular plan. Many people who have been at the same job for an extended period of time may not know much about the specifics of their pension plan. To find out important information that will help in your retirement planning, such as what type of plan you're covered by, what benefits you're entitled to, how much you'll receive at retirement, whether you'll receive payments or a lump sum, or whether your spouse is protected, consult your plan administrator and ask for a summary plan description, a summary annual report, and information about survivor coverage.

Most pension plans fall into one of the two following categories:

1) Defined benefit

2) Defined contribution

In the past, most employees were covered by a *defined benefit plan*. Upon retirement, they received a specified monthly benefit. Many plans paid a certain amount for each year of service. Some, however, paid a fixed dollar amount.

In recent years, the trend has been toward *defined contribution plans*, which do not promise to pay a predetermined benefit. Instead, the employer contributes a fixed amount to the employee's account (perhaps 5% of annual earnings). At retirement, the employee receives the total contribution, plus any investment returns, usually in a lump sum or annuity.

Individual Retirement Plans

Many employers have programs to help workers save for retirement. Often these "do-it-yourself" plans are offered in addition to regular pensions. In smaller companies, however, they may be the primary retirement program. In addition, you can create your own pension through contributions to a special account, whether your employer offers retirement benefits or not.

There are a few fundamental ground rules for saving efficiently:

- Savings must be disciplined and budgeted; they should be considered as important to the monthly budget as the mortgage payment or rent.
- Savings should be tax advantaged, which means they should be directed into tax-deductible, tax-deferred, or tax-free vehicles. An individual should first take advantage of all employer-sponsored plans, such as 401(k)s, SEP plans, SIMPLE plans, and then look to individual plans such as IRAs and Roth IRAs.

- Your savings should be allocated among various investments in order to safeguard and maximize returns, and reflect your investment strategy.

Individual Retirement Accounts

These plans have become increasingly more important in most thoughtful retirement plans since, more and more, retirees are requiring more retirement income to finance the life they want. These plans were designed to encourage individuals to save for their own retirement by allowing for taxdeferred accumulation of the retirement funds and, in some cases, tax deductibility of contributions to the plan. In 2017, workers can contribute up to $5,500 a year, and another $1,000 if they're fifty or older, and defer paying taxes on earnings from this money until they withdraw it. In some cases, all or part of the contribution is tax deductible. IRAs may be set up instead of or in addition to any pension plan your employer offers.

The rules for IRA distribution are strict. There is a 10% penalty for early withdrawal before age fifty-nine and a half, in addition to any tax owed on the income. Also, you must start distributions before age seventy and a half. To avoid penalties, these withdrawals cannot fall below a certain amount; the minimum amount is calculated each year by dividing your life expectancy, as reported in IRS mortality tables, into the total amount in your IRA. The idea is that all of your IRA contributions will be distributed during your lifetime. If you want to stretch withdrawals over a longer period, you can calculate minimum distributions using the joint life expectancy of yourself and your IRA's designated beneficiary.

You can invest IRA funds in almost anything: stocks, bonds, mutual funds, money market funds, and certificates of deposit are some of the more common options. On the other hand, commodity futures contracts, tangible personal property, art or antiques, gold and silver coins minted outside the US, and life insurance policies are not permitted for IRAs. To find out if your IRA contribution istax deductible, contact the IRS or your tax advisor.

Here again, the rules governing IRA contributions are likely to change as the government addresses Social Security reform and the larger issue of baby boomer retirees.

Following are twenty IRA tips to consider to help you get the most out of your IRA.

20 Tips to Get the Most from Your IRA

1. Individual Retirement Accounts

Once you've maxed out your employer's qualified retirement plan, it's time to consider an IRA. Traditional IRAs come in two flavors: deductible and nondeductible. Both offer tax-deferred growth. Roth IRAs, named for William J. Roth, their chief cheerleader in the US Senate, also come in two versions: regular and conversion. Both offer tax-free growth.

2. Traditional IRAs

Want an immediate tax deduction? Open an old-fashioned IRA. Be aware, though, that if you are covered by a retirement plan at work, an adjusted gross income (AGI) of $71,000 ($118,000 for a couple) will make you ineligible to make deductible contributions to an IRA. Not covered by a retirement plan where you work? Then it makes no difference how sizable your income is. You are eligible to make a deductible contribution.

However, to contribute to a traditional IRA, you do have to earn something. "Earned income," in this instance, includes taxable alimony but not nontaxable child support or unemployment compensation. And, of course, you must be younger than seventy and a half.

3. Spousal IRAs

Many couples who are ineligible for deductible IRAs can qualify for a spousal IRA. The AGI limit is considerably higher for a deductible contribution to a spousal IRA by someone who is not employed but whose spouse is covered by some kind of retirement plan. Currently, deductibility starts to phase out when AGI tops $184,001 and vanishes when it tops $194,000.

4. Deadline

You have until the day that IRS Form 1040 is due, April 15, to open an IRA and deposit your money, unless you file an extension.

5. Early withdrawals from an IRA

Not until you begin withdrawals is there a reckoning with the IRS. Withdrawals of earnings or deductible contributions are taxed as ordinary income. This applies even if your money was invested in tax-free municipal bonds, which is why you should never put such investments in an IRA.

Withdrawals made before you reach age fifty-nine and a half, though, are subject not only to the taxes that would ordinarily be due, but also to a penalty of 10% of the amount you're taking out. The penalty will not be charged if you die or are permanently disabled, or if you're withdrawing the money to pay for college, qualified medical expenses, health-insurance premiums while you're unemployed, to buy your first home, or if you take it out via 72(t) distribution.

6. Late IRA withdrawals

The IRS also imposes a penalty for late withdrawals from your IRA. This one kicks in if you fail to start taking out the minimum required amount of money by April 1 of the year following the year you turn seventy and a half. Minimum distributions for subsequent years must be made by Dec. 31. You can always remove funds faster than required, but failure to take at least the minimum means the IRS will hit you up for 50% of the difference between what you actually took and what you should have taken, which is a set amount based on your life expectancy or, if you so elect, the combined life expectancies of you and your spouse.

7. Don't delay that first distribution

It can prove costly to delay the first required distribution until April of the following year, even though you're allowed to. Suppose you turn seventy and a half in a calendar year, and put off the first withdrawal until the next calendar year. You will have to make a second withdrawal sometime in that calendar year, and the two combined could not only boost your income into a higher tax bracket, but also subject more of your Social Security payments to income tax.

8. Another reason not to delay

In addition, making two withdrawals that first year might cause you to forfeit a valuable tax benefit. Many states allow a sizable annual exclusion—meaning escape from taxes—for distributions from IRAs and other retirement plans. Delay your first withdrawal and you could lose that first year's exclusion.

9. Roth IRAs: The bad news

Contributions to a Roth IRA do not reduce your income for tax purposes, as they are made with after-tax dollars. But they do provide some serious advantages, as we'll see next.

10. Roth IRAs: The good news

For starters, you can withdraw money you contributed to your Roth account at any time for any reason without tax or penalty.

Earnings, too, are tax free, no matter how much an account has swelled, as long as you wait at least five years after opening the account and, generally, as long as you are at least fiftynine and a half. Unlike traditional IRAs, Roth withdrawals will not trigger taxes on otherwise tax-free Social Security benefits.

11. Eligibility

Another difference: Roth IRAs permit you to keep making contri-butions as long as you or your spouse has income from any kind of job. Income from investments is not included. However, you become

ineligible to make Roth contributions if your AGI tops $132,001
($194,001 when filing a joint return).

If you have a 401(k) and have contributed after-tax dollars to the
plan, a recent development may allow you to roll over your after-tax
portion to a Roth IRA when you leave your employment.

12. Roth conversions
You have the option of converting your traditional IRA into a Roth,
and thus avoiding taxes on any future withdrawals.

13. Roth conversions—tax issues
Such conversions come with a price tag. Assuming that all of the
money in your original IRA came from deductible contributions,
you will pay taxes on the entire amount you are converting to a Roth,
and you'll pay at your ordinary income rate, regardless of when you
opened the original IRA account.

14. Roth conversions—the route to redemption
This tax is due in the year you make the conversion, and a really
painful situation could arise if, by the time you come to pay your
taxes, stock prices and mutual fund NAVs are considerably lower than
they were when you made the conversion. You would then be paying
taxes on money you no longer have.

Fortunately, the Roth rules offer an escape hatch. Should the above
situation arise, simply reverse your conversion back to a traditional
IRA, and then reconvert the now smaller amount back to a new
Roth. This tactic can save you thousands of dollars, but be aware that
regulations permit only one such re-conversion per year.

15. Removing Roth money

Unlike the rigid withdrawal schedules for traditional IRAs, Roths do not require you to start removing money when you reach any particular age. The funds can stay there until you die. Your unspent Roth money will then belong to your beneficiaries and, depending on who they are, can continue to grow tax free. Be aware, though, that if your beneficiary is anyone other than your spouse, he or she will have to comply with a minimum-distribution requirement.

16. Should you convert?

The advantages of a Roth are compelling, but the account is not for everyone. To determine if it's right for you, you need to explore several questions, even though some of the answers will be little more than intelligent guesses about the future.

For example, you might be better off with a traditional account if you expect your tax bracket to drop once you stop working. In making the Roth/traditional determination, plug in variables that can change the answer, such as the age at which you expect to stop working.

17. Nondeductible traditional IRAs

Even if your AGI is too high to permit you to open a traditional IRA or a Roth, you can still stash a nondeductible $5,500 a year, plus $1,000 catch-up if you are fifty years old or older, in a traditional IRA. The money you earn on such contributions will accumulate tax-free until withdrawals start, at which point it will be taxed as ordinary income. Contributions made in nondeductible, after-tax dollars will not be taxed upon withdrawal, but the law treats all withdrawals—regardless of where the money originally came from—as having come proportionately from deductible and nondeductible contributions. The good news is that you can move money out of the nondeductible account and into a conversion Roth.

18. The nightmare of Form 8606

As you might imagine, calculating taxes on withdrawals gets complicated. To make matters worse, you will have to file an IRS Form 8606 every year in which you make a nondeductible contribution or withdraw money from an IRA to which nondeductible contributions have been made. This form will become very familiar to you because you'll also have to fill it out for any year in which you:

- Convert part or all of the assets in a traditional IRA to a Roth IRA or the reverse;
- Receive distributions from a Roth IRA; or
- Receive distributions from a traditional IRA, if you have ever made a nondeductible contribution to any of your traditional IRAs.

Translation: Hang on to the 8606 forms until you completely remove the money from all of your traditional IRAs, a process that could take decades.

19. Penalty for noncompliance

To really twist the knife, the law authorizes the IRS to exact a $50 penalty if you do not file a required Form 8606, unless you are able to prove that the failure was due to reasonable cause. Be advised that, according to the IRS, the disease known as "formophobia" is *not* reasonable cause.

20. IRAs and estate taxes

Confusion abounds about the interplay of income taxes and estate taxes. For estate tax purposes, all IRA funds, whether housed in traditional or Roth accounts, count as part of your taxable estate, subject, at your death, to taxes of up to 40 percent. Fortunately, the ceiling on the amount of money you can pass on to your beneficiaries before these taxes kick in is rising. Spouses can receive an unlimited amount of assets, and other beneficiaries can inherit up to $5,450,000 before they have to give the government a cut.

One area that gets overlooked is income taxes on inherited IRAs. The good news is a surviving spouse doesn't have to pay income taxes on an inherited IRA from a deceased spouse, provided the money is kept in the deceased's IRA or rolled over to the surviving spouse's IRA. However, beyond that, all of the proceeds from an IRA are subject to state and federal income taxes. This can be as high as 39.60% from a federal level plus state income taxes, if applicable. This can lead to almost half of your IRA vanishing. I'll address in chapter 10 a way to prevent this from happening.

401(k) Plans

401(k) plans have become enormously popular. The way they work is that you can defer paying taxes on a portion of your salary by contributing it to a special account set up by your employer called a 401(k) plan. Tax isn't due on the money until it's withdrawn, usually at retirement. Companies often impose a ceiling on contributions, and the government sets another limit of $18,000 plus a $6,000 makeup provision if you're fifty or older. Employers often chip in some matching percentage.

The rules for distribution of 401(k)s are similar to those for IRAs: you can withdraw funds without penalty after age fiftynine and a half or at retirement, and you must start withdrawing by age seventy and a half.

Roth 401(k) Plans

Some employer 401(k) plans offer a Roth component. This allows the employee to choose where they want their contributions applied— pretax or after tax, or both—providing the sum of the two do not exceed today's limits.

Employee Stock Ownership Plans (ESOP)

Many companies have implemented stock ownership plans for employees. Indeed, many Microsoft and Google employees became millionaires because of this type of plan. A company, through a trust it establishes, purchases shares of its own stock for employees. The trust holds the stock in individual employee accounts and distributes it to workers. You may not have to pay tax on them until you receive a distribution from the trust, typically at retirement when your tax rate may be lower.

Annuities

Annuities are often purchased as a source of retirement income, and are available through life insurance companies. They allow you to invest money, either as a lump payment or in installments, and receive a certain sum each month for life in return. I discuss these in greater detail later in the book.

Chapter Three:

Know Your Social Security Options

One of the most common questions we get from our clients is, "When should we sign up to start receiving our Social Security benefits?"

Our answer is always, "It depends."

It depends on one's health, needs, and resources.

The first step is to know your full retirement age, or FRA. If you were born between 1943 and 1954, your full retirement age is sixty-six. You must add two months for 1955 and each year after that, and if you were born in 1960 or later, your full retirement age is sixty-seven.

If you were born in...	Your full retirement age is
1943-1954	66
1955	66 and 2 months
1956	66 and 4 months
1957	66 and 6 months
1958	66 and 8 months
1959	66 and 10 months
1960 or later	67

Much has been written about the benefits of waiting to start collecting your benefits. It's true that for each year you wait to start collecting your benefits, the higher your benefits will be. The earliest that you can begin collecting your retirement benefits is age sixty-two. For each year that you wait, your benefits will increase by 7% up to your full retirement age. From your full retirement age to age seventy, your benefits go up by 8% per year. Beyond age seventy your benefits do not increase by waiting. In my example below, I'm assuming that a retiree at full retirement age would receive $2,000 per month in Social Security income. At age sixty-two, that benefit would be $1,500 per month. If the retiree waits to start collecting benefits at age seventy, the benefit would be $2,640 per month.

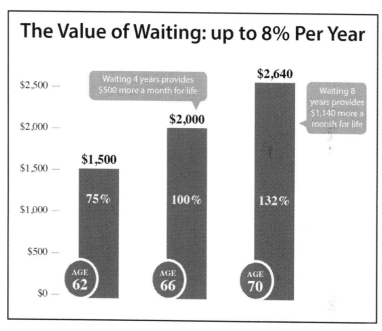

Initially, it certainly appears that waiting to collect benefits makes good sense; however, waiting means that you'll need to use more of your personal resources.

Another way to look at it is this: each year that you delay your benefit is a year that you won't be receiving Social Security. Using the same numbers from my previous example, the amount of money that the retiree would *not* have received from ages sixty-two through sixty-six is $72,000. From ages sixty-six through seventy the amount *not* received is $96,000, and from age sixty-two through age seventy the amount is $144,000. If the retiree delays claiming his benefit, the breakeven point in all three examples is around age eighty-one, on average. The graph below illustrates what I mean.

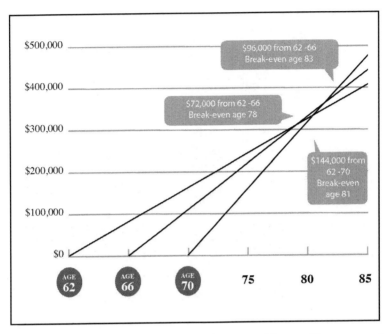

Another consideration is whether you're working and have earned income prior to your full retirement age. This is especially important because it can have an effect on your benefits. If you are not at your full retirement age and have earned income in excess of $15,720, Social Security will hold back $1 for every $2 that you are over the limit.

In the year that you *reach* your full retirement age, but before you *actually turn* your full retirement age, Social Security will withhold $1 for every $3 that you are over the limit of $41,880. The good news is that after your full retirement age, there is no limit on your earnings.

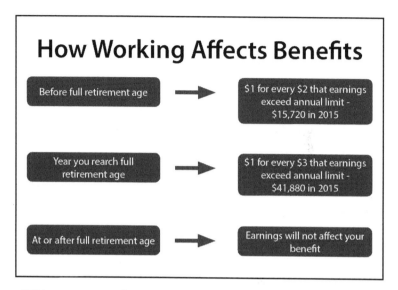

With so many options to consider, you will want to fully analyze your options before making a decision. Another consideration should include your feelings about the future of Social Security. I think there is a good chance that Social Security will not keep up with inflation, and you shouldn't rule out a reduction in future benefits. Note, if Social Security goes bankrupt, payments would still continue, but most likely at a reduced amount.

On the subject of Social Security, I think a better understanding of the history of this venerable institution is important. From its beginnings, this government program had good intentions; however, with good intentions often come problems.

The History of Social Security

Social Security is over eighty years old, and over the years it has provided varying levels of assistance to a great many Americans. But when planning ahead, it's important to understand what Social Security promises and what it doesn't.

In August of 2005, Franklin Delano Roosevelt's grandson, James Roosevelt Jr., who is also a former associate commissioner of the Social Security Administration, wrote a guest commentary that appeared in many newspapers around the country. According to Mr. Roosevelt, one in five retirees relies upon Social Security as their *only* source of income. Today, over sixty-five million people receive Social Security benefits.

Unfortunately, the impending exodus of the baby boomers from the workforce presents actuarial issues that, if not addressed soon, will create financial pressure on the system. It's worth taking a closer look at an aging program that was the hallmark of FDR's New Deal.

On June 8, 1934, Franklin Delano Roosevelt gave a speech to Congress announcing his plans for a landmark new "American program" that would insure "the security of men, women and children of the Nation against certain hazards and vicissitudes of life." This bold new program—"Social Security," as it became known—was met with great enthusiasm. For a country in the throes of a debilitating economic depression, it was both a practical measure to a desperate situation and a bright, shining symbol of the burgeoning great nation that, despite its then-current economic woes (shared to a large extent by the rest of the world), was developing into a superpower—economically, militarily, and morally. The bold new American program would be the cornerstone of a grand social vision that FDR would call his New Deal. And Americans took a great deal of pride in that idea. The grand vision was worthy of the grand nation Americans saw themselves becoming.

Over the next year the details of the system were debated and hashed out; and as this happened, the president gave regular updates to Congress and the American people. In an address to Congress in January of 1935, FDR laid out various elements of the plan. The Social Security system would involve a dedicated tax on income that would be collected from American workers. As Americans reached retirement age, they would be paid benefits to provide for their needs in old age. The system was set up so current workers would pay the benefits of current retirees. (At the time, there were about forty workers for each retiree.) The surplus would go into a Social Security trust fund administered by trustees in the Treasury of the United States, and was to be used when the system encountered "rainy days."

To be precise, there are two Social Security trust funds: the Old-Age and Survivors Insurance (OASI) and the Disability Insurance (DI) Trust Funds. Benefits to retired workers and their families, and to families of deceased workers, are paid from the OASI Trust Fund. Benefits to disabled workers and their families are paid from the DI Trust Fund. More than 98% of total disbursements from the combined OASI and DI funds in 2014 were for benefit payments. Most people simply refer to them together as the "trust fund."

In that address, the president declared that "sound financial management of the funds and the reserves, and protection of the credit structure of the Nation, should be assured by retaining Federal control over all funds through trustees in the Treasury of the United States."

Despite reservations from some who believed the surplus would be much too big and, consequently, too much of a temptation for future administrations who, in the throes of economic mismanagement, would dip into the trust fund to extricate themselves politically from budget woes, the legislation was passed in Congress. Then on August 14, 1935, FDR signed the bold new American program—Social Security—into law.

Over the next sixty years, millions of Americans benefited from that grand vision that rose up out of the ashes of the Great Depression. The program has been an unqualified success and a great source of pride by most Americans who have seen it as a pillar of the greatest society in the history of the world, and perhaps the greatest achievement of a president and his administration, universally acknowledged as one of the greatest in American history.

Pressure on the Social Security Trust Fund

Unfortunately, over the years many administrations did not heed the warning that FDR issued concerning the sound financial management of the Social Security trust fund.

While great surpluses built up, economic crises over the years have sent lesser administrations eager to improve their poll numbers and chances for reelection dipping into the trust fund for temporary bailouts to economic problems. The result is that the trust fund has been raided many times over the years without repaying the sums that were supposedly "borrowed," using the rationale that it is so large that the fund can absorb these "withdrawals."

As I mentioned earlier, when Social Security legislation was passed in 1935, there were about forty workers per each retiree. At the turn of the millennium when I wrote *The Master Plan*, those numbers had dropped to three workers per each retiree. Today we have only 2.9 workers per retiree, and this amount is expected to drop to two workers per retiree by 2030 as thousands of baby boomers retire daily and begin to collect Social Security benefits. This statistic is significant because the baby boomer generation—those born between 1946 and 1964—constitutes the largest generation in the history of the United States. The population explosion that started when GIs came home from World War II and lasted, for all intents and purposes, until the Viet Nam War, and the subsequent aging of that generation, was precisely the sort of scenario for which the trust fund was set up. As the vast numbers of baby boomers begin retiring, not only will there be increased strain on the system's trust fund to meet the benefit payments, but the number of people who contribute to the fund will be drastically reduced. Today Social Security is paying out more than it is taking in. The time has come that Congress needs to take serious action to fix our system.

According to the latest Social Security Trustee report, the trust fund may be depleted by 2033, which is twenty years sooner than the projections made in 1990. There is no doubt that the trust fund is being exhausted much faster than predicted. Currently Social Security is telling us that if or when the reserves are depleted, they should be able to pay about 76% of the scheduled benefits, due to taxes still being collected.

From the very beginning of Social Security, the intention was for it to be *supplementary* social insurance. FDR repeatedly made this clear to both Congress and the American people. He also made it clear that the government—not private individuals—should be responsible for the management of the funds paid into the program so as to avoid unsavory and usurious practices by what was then (as now) a too-frequently unscrupulous financial community.

There has been much discussion on how to strengthen Social Security. One of the ideas is to remove income limits, thus making 100% of earned income subject to FICA taxes. Another is to increase the amount that we pay in FICA taxes. Another idea is to push out the full retirement age. Another is to do means testing, which would mean limiting benefits to those who may not need it or who have saved for retirement and therefore have a robust retirement income. No matter what is decided, I'm sure many people will not be happy with the outcome.

The silver lining to the drain on the Social Security trust fund is that it exposes the fiction that the program doesn't need reform because it is fully backed by tax contributions. Lawmakers have many policy options to choose from to help fix the system. The only bad option is to do nothing at all, which would lead to reduced benefits and more debt. Consequently, it behooves ordinary Americans to take the bull by the horns and take responsibility for their own retirements.

In the following chapters, I'll reveal how to do just that.

Chapter Four:

Understanding Your Employer's Pension Plan Options

In the same way that Social Security has been the backbone of a public social insurance program for American workers and has been the source of a great amount of pride, employer pension plans have been the backbone of private retirement scenarios and have elicited as much pride and loyalty in the companies that sponsor them.

Unfortunately, in recent years many pension plans have been defaulted on because of their sponsors' financial woes.

Actually, our current political climate that allows companies to simply walk away from the promises they made to employees when they hired them is rooted in policies implemented in 1963 when, after sixty years of doing business, the Studebaker Corporation, the venerable carmaker, declared bankruptcy and junked the promised pensions of four thousand workers.

"You may be a long way from retirement age now," the company's brochure passed out to new employees had assured them. "Still it's good to know that Studebaker is building up a fund for you, so that when you reach retirement age you can settle down on a farm, visit around the country or just take it easy, and know that you'll still be getting a regular monthly pension paid for entirely by the company."

In 1974, Congress responded to this new trend of companies walking away from their pension obligations by writing and passing the Employee Retirement Income Security Act (ERISA), which established minimum standards for retirement plans in private industry, and created the Pension Benefit Guaranty Corporation (PBGC) to guarantee them. In truth, ERISA was riddled with loopholes that allowed corporations to raid their own pension funds and then rely on the PBGC—a taxpayer-funded government agency—to bail them out when they got into financial trouble.

The problem is that the PBGC pays only a fraction of the actual value of the pension plans of bankrupt companies that were due regular employees. Perhaps most disturbing of all is that the way the rules were written, executives and high-level managers received the lion's share of PBGC settlements, leaving regular employees with literally pennies on the dollars that were due them.

Take, for instance, the case of Leo Mullin, the former chairman and CEO of Delta Airlines. While Mullin was head of Delta, he killed the company's defined benefit plan and replaced it with a less generous plan. Two years after his retirement in 2003, the company went into bankruptcy, and the bankruptcy court determined that Delta could not reorganize or emerge from Chapter 11 unless the Delta

Pilots Retirement Plan (Pilot Plan) was terminated. Mullin was fine, though—he received a $16 million retirement package. This was calculated on roughly twenty-eight years of employment with Delta, which was twenty-one more than he actually worked.

The list of companies that have walked away from their pension obligations under the protection of bankruptcy reads like a who's who of American business: Pan Am Airlines, United Airlines, Delta Airlines, Northwest Airlines, US Airways, Bethlehem Steel, Delphi (GM), Polaroid, and on and on. Other venerable, perennial "blue chip" companies that no longer offer pension plans because of the costs include Hewlett-Packard, IBM, NCR, Sears, Motorola, and more virtually every day. When the dust is settled, the American taxpayers are left to pick up the pieces and pay the pensions that the corporations promised to pay but, when things got tight, decided not to. Ironically, many of the taxpayers who are having to pay the defaulted pensions don't even have pensions themselves!

Later in the chapter I'll take a look at some things you can do to stay on top of your pension situation and, should your company declare bankruptcy and default on its pension plan, get the most out of the limited federal insurance that covers such occurrences. But first, let's take a look at the plans themselves.

Two Types of Pensions

Upon retirement, many workers continue to receive monetary compensation from their employer in the form of a pension. There are mainly two types of pensions: **defined benefit plans** and **defined contribution plans**.

Under a defined benefit plan—once common but now rarely used—the benefit that an employee receives is normally based on the length of a worker's employment and the wages that were received. Each employee does not have a separate account in these programs, as the money to support the pensions is generally administered through a trust established by the employer.

In a defined contribution plan, the employer makes regular deposits into an account established for each employee. During retirement, the employee is not guaranteed to receive a given amount but only the amount actually in the account.

Pensions are governed primarily by federal statutory law. As noted earlier, in 1974 Congress passed the Employee Retirement Income Security Act (ERISA) under its constitutional mandate to regulate interstate commerce. The act was passed in response to the mismanagement of funds in direct benefit plans. All employers who engage in interstate commerce and provide defined benefit plans to their employees must abide by ERISA guidelines.

The provisions of ERISA do *not* apply to defined contribution plans.

ERISA is highly complicated and provides detailed regulations for many aspects of defined contribution plans. ERISA requires that employers provide both the Labor Department and its employees with detailed descriptions of the benefits they are to receive. It also outlines which employees must receive a pension if they are offered, and requires that a percentage of the retirement benefits become vested in the employees after they have worked for a given number of years and/or have reached a given age. ERISA also requires that pension plans provide benefits to an employee's survivors upon her death. The legislation also requires employers to adequately fund the program, and establishes fiduciary responsibilities that must be adhered to. ERISA also establishes the Pension Benefit Guaranty Corporation (PBGC) to insure defined benefits plans. Employers must pay premiums so that their plans are covered by the PBGC. The termination of plans is also extensively regulated.

To encourage employers to provide pension plans that follow congressionally established guidelines such as ERISA, Congress has authorized tax breaks to employers who follow the guidelines. Title 26 of the Internal Revenue Code establishes numerous qualifications and requirements in order for an employer to receive special tax treatment.

Summary of Qualified Plans

As I mentioned, the Employee Retirement Income Security Act (ERISA) of 1974 ushered in a new era in retirement planning. ERISA established new rules and strict standards for employer-sponsored retirement plans, including guidelines for employee coverage, funding, and contributions. Not only did it add much-needed structure to employee pension plans, but it also increased the amount of paperwork for plan sponsors and administrators. The result is that many employers reconsidered their retirement plan strategies and, because they required much less paperwork, the popularity of defined contribution plans increased.

Retirement plans that meet all the Internal Revenue Code (IRC) requirements may qualify for favorable tax treatment provided through the IRC. These plans entitle employers to realize immediate benefits in the form of tax-deductible contributions, and future tax benefits through the tax plan's tax-deferred earnings.

In today's competitive labor market, most employers offer some sort of retirement plan in order to attract the best employees. They also are usually interested in realizing as many benefits for themselves as possible, generally getting tax breaks on contributions paid and structuring the plan so that the owner and other key employees benefit most. ERISA limits how much owners can favor their key employees and still qualify for favorable tax treatment. Nonetheless, owners tend to maximize their benefit by choosing a plan that best suits the owners' needs.

Good retirement plans can boost morale, increase productivity by keeping quality employees with the company for longer, and enhance loyalty. However, the bottom-line financial benefits to the company are almost always the driving force behind whatever plan is offered.

For the most part, an employer retirement plan must meet the following requirements in order to qualify for favorable tax treatment:

- It must be established by the employer for the exclusive benefit of employees and their beneficiaries;
- It must be permanent in nature;
- It must be in writing and communicated to all current employees;
- It must be financed or funded by the employer, the employees, or both;

- It must provide contributions and benefits that are not discriminatory under ERISA or IRC rules;
- It must comply with contribution and benefit limits guidelines;
- It must comply with regulations affecting minimum participation and coverage;
- There must be separation from the sponsor's general assets, vesting, funding, disclosure, and more.

These requirements are intended to ensure that qualified plans do not discriminate in favor of highly compensated employees and that they are operated in a financially sound manner.

Tax Advantages of Qualified Pension Plans

With a qualified plan, an employer can provide benefits to employees under conditions that reduce current taxes for both parties.

Advantages include:

- The employer's contribution is generally deductible in the year it is made, assuming that the contribution is made no later than the date on which the employer's income tax—including extensions—is filed;
- Expenses incurred to establish and maintain the qualified plan are considered to be deductible business expenses to the employer;
- The employer's contribution to the plan on behalf of the employee is not included in the employee's current income;

- Earnings or gains from investments held in qualified plans accumulate tax free until they are actually distributed to plan participants (this includes earnings attributable to employee contributions);
- Employee contributions can reduce an employee's personal taxes by reducing the amount of his or her taxable income.

A Nutshell Comparison of the Two Types of Plans

Defined Contribution (more common today):
- Specifies the contributions made on an employee's behalf.
- Has individual employee accounts.
- May be funded entirely by the employer, but usually includes employee contributions.
- Cannot provide for past service.
- Costs are predictable.
- Generally favors younger employees.
- Relatively simple to administer.
- Relatively easy to explain to employees.

Defined Benefit (less common today):
- Specifies the benefits an employee receives at retirement.
- No individual accounts; assets are lumped together.
- Usually paid fully by the employer.
- Can provide for past service.
- Costs can be unpredictable.
- Can benefit older workers (based on final earnings).

- Relatively cumbersome and expensive to administer.
- Can be difficult to explain to employees.

If you have a defined benefit plan, you'll be asked to make an irrevocable decision when you retire that will affect you and your spouse if married.

The decision that you'll be making is how you want to receive your benefits. The following are the more common options:

Single Life—This option provides the highest level of benefit; however, the benefit terminates at the death of the retiree.

Survivor—There are a number of variations of survivor benefits under this option. There will be a reduction of benefit, and the amount will depend on which option you choose. The most common options are 50%, 75%, and 100% benefit to the surviving spouse. The higher the benefit, the greater the reduction of benefit for the retiree. Some pensions provide additional options such as period certain. As an example, a "ten-year-certain" option will provide a beneficiary ten years of benefit minus the number of years that the retiree received the benefit.

Lump sum—Some pensions offer their retirees an option to take a lump sum rather than an annuity. Retirees need to analyze how much they think they can earn if they are considering this option and determine if it will provide the income that they would have received under one of the above options or at the very least the income that they'll need. The retiree also needs to be disciplined with a lump sum and not treat the amount like a piggy bank. Remember, this money needs to last your lifetime.

If the retiree chooses this option, the retiree needs to have the money rolled over to an IRA. Failure to do so will result in a taxable event. Before making your selection, I recommend that you start with an income analysis. This analysis should consider your direct income sources under various scenarios, such as what your financial picture would look like in the event of death.

Next, consider your health. If you have health issues and are married, you may want to consider which option will provide the most benefit to your spouse. I think that it's a good idea to have an exam done before deciding.

How about the health of your pension? Is it fully funded or does it have huge deficits? The first step is to assess your company's financial health. A healthy company cannot simply hand its pension obligations to the government and walk away. The company must be in bankruptcy to default on its pension obligations, and even then it must convince a federal bankruptcy judge that such a step is necessary.

If your company is a publically traded company, it's much easier to find financial information on its financial health. You can find a wealth of information by going to Google or your favorite investment research services such as Morningstar or Standard & Poor.

If the company's finances show signs of weakness, it makes sense to try to determine the strength of the pension. This may take a lot more work because pension documents can be cryptic. If your company offers a pension, they must file an annual report with the Labor Department. The section called Schedule B, Actuarial Information, is most relevant.

These reports may be obtained from the administrator of your company's pension or from the Office of Public Disclosure at the Labor Department.

401(k) Plans

Today there are many different types of corporate retirement plans, most of which are some form of a defined contribution plan. One of the most popular defined contribution plan is the 40l(k) plan, which can stand alone or operate in conjunction with another type of defined contribution plan, including the most common type, a profit-sharing plan, as well as stock bonus plan, thrift plan, or money-purchase plan established prior to the enactment of ERISA. (Some of the newer money-purchase plans may not have 401(k) provisions.)

An employee can take part of his or her salary in cash, with an immediate tax liability, or defer a portion of their salary by having it directed into a 401(k) account. Employee contributions are regarded not as payments by them, but as the deferral of salary. The immediate tax advantage to an employee is derived not from tax-deductible contributions, but from a reduction in income tax because of a reduction in salary.

In 2017, the maximum annual amount that an employee can defer into the plan, known as the elective contribution or elective deferral, is $18,000.

Elective deferrals by the employee are tax-deductible to the employer. Like wages, the amounts deferred are subject to Social Security (FICA) taxation and federal unemployment (FUTA) tax.

Elective employee contributions in the form of salary reductions are 100% vested from the moment they are made. Requirements may stipulate that a certain percentage be deferred as a condition of participation, but most do not because it may lead to discriminatory contributions favoring the highly paid. Many employers provide matching contributions that are pegged to the employee's elective deferral percentage or amount. Lower-paid employees have an increased incentive to participate in the plan when an employer offers a matching contribution. This is key, since nondiscrimination rules require that a minimum percentage of rank-and-file employees elect to participate in the plan in order for key employees to participate. Increasing the rankand-file employees' incentive to participate can do much to prevent disqualification of the plan.

Catch-up Provisions for Older Participants

Those who participate in certain defined contribution plans such as 401(k)s, and are at least fifty years old, can increase their annual elective deferrals. This allows them to save even more for retirement. In 2017, the amount is $6,000. The catch-up deferrals are available even if other restrictions apply.

Take Advantage of Company Matching!

Many employers match an employee's 401(k) contributions up to a certain percentage of their salary. I'm amazed how many employees don't contribute any money or less than an employer's match. If this describes you, you are passing up on free money.

According to the Financial Industry Regulatory Authority (FINRA), 26.9% of 401(k) participants do contribute enough to receive their full employer's match. This number is even higher among younger workers. Your 401(k) can be a powerful resource for building a secure retirement, and an employer's match can add a substantial amount to your retirement nest egg. Let's say that you are forty years old earning $50,000 annually and contribute 4% of your earnings to your 401(k) and you have an annual average rate of return of 7%. To keep things simple, let's assume that you never receive a pay raise. By the time you are sixty-five you would have contributed $50,000. Add in the annual 7% rate of return and you'd be sitting on $135,352. Now let's say that your employer has a 4% match, which adds another $50,000 into your plan over the same twenty-five years. The sum now goes to $270,705! Now that is a great deal, isn't it?

As a side note, your employer's matching to your 401(k) doesn't count toward your maximum contribution limits. There is, however, a combined limit of $59,000 between the employee and employer.

In addition to offering the potential for free money through a match, you receive significant tax advantages. Using the above scenario, let's say that you are in a 25% tax bracket. This would mean rather than receiving $48,000 after your $2,000 annual contribution, you would be receiving $48,500! In other words you'd be saving $500 in taxes each year.

A growing number of employers offer a 401(k) option, where employees make contributions with after-tax money. You don't receive the immediate tax savings, but the major selling point is that your withdrawals are tax free. Keep in mind that the IRS requires an employer's matching dollars reside in a pretax portion of your 401(k).

Big 401(k) Match Mistake!

Are you getting the most from your employer's matching? Did you know that if you max out your contributions to your 401(k) prior to the end of the year, you may not be getting your employer's full matching?

Most employers do their matching on a payroll basis, contributing a little bit with each paycheck if the employee is making contributions as well. Here's an example. Dave, a forty-nine-year-old employee earning $100,000, fully funds his 401(k) by the end of September, without considering how his employer matches. His employer provides a 5% match, so through the end of September his employer contributes $3,749 to his 401(k). However, his employer does not do any matching from November through the end of the year because Dave wasn't making any contributions. That means that he left $1,251 on the table. Ouch!

Most 401(k) plans operate like my example above, but not all. It pays to know how your employer matches and how your plan works so that you don't make the same mistake as Dave.

Should You Roll Over Your 401(k) to an IRA?

If you have a 401(k) or some other retirement plan with a previous employer, you have the option to roll over your retirement savings to an IRA or possibly leave it with your former employer.

When leaving an employer, whether voluntary or involuntary, many experts believe there are advantages to rolling over your retirement savings to an IRA. However, you should study your options and the advantages and disadvantages of each.

Some of the key advantages include:

Control—As the owner of your IRA, you have complete control versus being dependent upon the rules and policies of your former employer's retirement plan, including partial or full distributions.

Investment flexibility—More than likely your previous employer's plan has a limited number of investment options to choose from. A rollover to an IRA will open the door to a universe of many investment options.

Professional money managers—Most likely you are getting limited investment advice from your previous employer's plan provider. Rolling your retirement savings to an IRA will give you the opportunity to have a professional money manager manage the monies for you based on your goals and needs.

Estate-planning benefits—An IRA will allow your heirs to receive the benefit over their life expectancy, thus not getting hit with a large tax liability like they would if they withdrew the monies in a lump sum. Some employer plans allow this as well.

Consolidation—It's easier to manage all your investments and your eventual required minimum distributions from one account.

Some disadvantages of rolling over your retirement savings to an IRA include:

Higher expenses—Contrary to what you may think, your employer's plan has expenses; however, IRAs may have higher expenses. If this is the case, you should consider what you are getting for the higher fees. Ultimately the bottom line is net results after expenses on a risk-adjusted basis.

Early access—Your employer's plan may allow penalty-free withdrawals prior to age fifty-nine and a half. Typically you can take a penalty-free withdrawal from an employer's plan after you reach fifty-five. With that said, you can withdraw money penalty free from an IRA prior to fifty-nine and a half if you follow the IRS rule IRC 72(t), which states that your withdrawals need to be based on life expectancy for a minimum of five years. After the five years is satisfied, you can alter the amount of your withdrawal.

Wolves in sheep's clothing—Every financial salesperson is going to want to be your best friend when they know that you may have a sum of money available to move. They will try their best to convince you that they have the best product. You must do your homework if you decide to work with someone. I've dedicated a chapter to help you choose the right advisor.

Chapter Five:

Making Sure Your Money Lasts as Long as You Do

Of all the financial decisions you'll have to make in your lifetime of investing, none will be more important and more challenging than how to invest your retirement savings during your retirement years. Think about it: you want an income to supplement your other retirement income sources, such as Social Security and perhaps a pension; you want it to keep up with inflation; and you want it to last no matter how long you live. The problem is how to meet all of these goals at the same time.

In this chapter we are going to examine investment options and explain the factors that can affect performance, lower volatility, and create an income that lasts a lifetime.

Speaking of a lifetime, how long is a lifetime? Interestingly enough, the longer you live, the longer you are expected to live.

Paying for retirement is increasingly becoming more of a do-it-yourself proposition. Fewer companies are offering pensions. Instead, companies are offering 401(k)-type plans, which shift much of the burden of providing employees with a guaranteed retirement income from the employer to the employee. This means that employees will need to learn to invest their retirement savings in such a way that will allow them to withdraw from their accounts with reasonable confidence so they don't deplete their nest egg too soon.

To successfully set up your distribution plan, you'll need to make some important assumptions, such as how much income you think you'll need, how long you think you'll need it, and how you think your investments will perform.

There is no one-plan-fits-all because everyone's situation is unique. I will, however, discuss various approaches to help answer the question: "How much can I withdraw each year and be confident that my money will last a lifetime?"

Let's say you withdraw a fixed amount of between 4 and 5 percent of a portfolio's value in the first year, and then adjust it upward each year by whatever the inflation rate was the previous year.

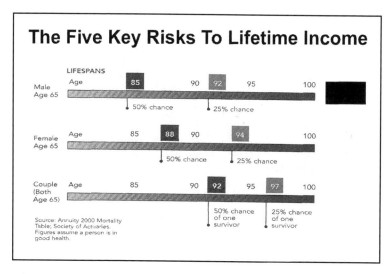

As an example, if you retire with $500,000 and withdraw 5%, you'd end up with a $25,000 withdrawal in the first year. If the previous year's inflation rate was 3%, you'd increase the next year's withdraw rate by $750, for a total withdraw of $25,750 in year two, $26,522 in year three, and so on.

The problem with this idea is that steadily increasing your withdrawals can lead to disaster in a prolonged bear market. If you are not careful, you can quickly devour your portfolio, leaving you with little or no money to carry you through the rest of your life.

Sequence of Returns Risk

The best-case scenario is to retire into a bull market where there will be a string of positive years with returns greater than your withdrawal rate. However, retiring at the beginning of a bear market where you have multiple negative years right off the bat can be extremely detrimental to your retirement accounts if you are taking withdrawals.

See the following two graphs that illustrate my point.

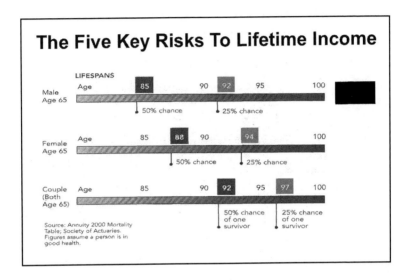

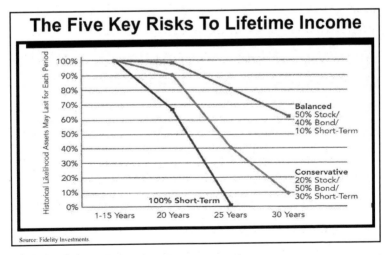

Next, instead of withdrawing a fixed dollar amount, I'd recommend

using a percentage. I like using a withdrawal rate of 4%, but instead of converting that to a fixed dollar amount, simply leave it as an annual percentage. Let's go back to the previous example of retiring with $500,000. This time you withdraw 4% annually. This would give you an annual income of $20,000, or $1,666 monthly.

If your account goes up, say, 2% net of the previous year's withdrawal, your next year's withdrawal would be $20,400, or $1,700 monthly. On the other hand, if your account decreased 2%, your next year's withdrawal would be $19,600, or $1,633 monthly.

While your income will vary some with this method, your chances of running out of money will be virtually eliminated.

This method comes with an automatic braking system. In a big market decline like we saw in 2008, you're forced to cut back your spending, which in turn limits the damage that you'd inflict on your portfolio. In years that the market does well and you have a little extra cash flow, you should salt a little of it away into your savings account to give you some cushion during years when cash flow could be down.

Another consideration is from where you will take your distributions. I recommend using the cheapest month first. As an example, we know any withdrawals taken from a qualified account such as an IRA will be subject to ordinary income taxes, whereas money taken from a nonqualified account, such as a savings account, is not. More than likely, if your IRA is invested in a diversified equity portfolio, you are averaging a much higher return than what you are earning in a savings account. So, in this case I would withdraw money from my savings since there won't be taxes on withdrawals, and the earnings are more than likely much less than an IRA. Keep in mind that it's a good idea to keep a good cash reserve for emergencies and future purchases. I like to see six to twelve months of expenses kept in savings. Maybe you don't have a significant amount of cash, but you have two IRAs. Since withdrawals from either IRA are going to be taxable, I would select the IRA with the lowest returns to take the withdrawals from. Maybe you have two similar investment accounts with similar returns, but one is an IRA and the other account is not. In this case, I would take the money from the non-IRA account. Even if there are some taxes, most likely the taxes will be lower because 100% of the withdrawals from the IRA will be taxes as ordinary income taxes vs. capital gains rates.

There are numerous scenarios depending on what type of accounts you have to withdraw from. If you have taxable savings and investment accounts, as well as tax-deferred accounts like an IRA and possibly a Roth IRA which are tax free, it would be wise to develop a withdraw strategy to minimize taxes and maximize withdrawals.

Dividends Are a Retiree's Best Friend

Even though I'm neither retired nor currently need the income, I love dividends. I love dividends because dividends are substantially more dependable and predictable than share prices. While I'm confident that the share prices of the companies that we own will go up over time, I have no idea if share prices of the stock I own will go up or down from day to day.

I love dividends more than the interest that CDs and bonds provide. A good strategy is to invest in companies that have a history of increasing their dividends; CDs and bonds don't.

Ideally, if dividends can meet your income requirements, you'll never need to sell shares in order to cover your withdrawals. This becomes even more important during a market decline.

The withdrawal needs of many retirees may exceed the dividends being paid, which means that some amount of shares will need to be sold to cover their withdrawal requirements. If this is your case, I encourage you to lower your withdrawals so that your dividends cover 50%, or hopefully more, of your withdrawal needs.

I will talk more about dividends in the next chapter.

Guaranteed Income for Life

Probably because I understand investments and probabilities, I'm confident with income strategies like withdrawing a fixed percentage based on the balance of my account or focusing on dividends.

However, if you lose sleep over the ups and downs of the market and fear that you may outlive your income, I have good news for you. There are insurance solutions (annuities) that provide lifetime income guarantees. These income guarantees come at a cost, however; if having an income guarantee helps you to sleep better at night, you might find the cost to be worth all the tea in China. I will cover annuities in more detail in the next chapter.

Taking Early Retirement Distributions without Penalties—IRC 72(t)

Are you facing a layoff? Considering early retirement? If so, this chapter may be especially important. Managing your finances can be a real balancing act even while you are working, let alone when you're unemployed. The time may come when your immediate financial needs will take priority over longer-term savings goals. If so, there's a good chance that your largest source of available money is your retirement plan at your former job. If this is the case, you could cash in your plan. However, by doing so you may face severe consequences.

First of all, if you're under age fifty-nine and a half, you may need to pay a 10% premature withdrawal penalty to the IRS.

Second, you'll be paying current income taxes. You may even find yourself in a higher tax bracket due to the distribution amount.

Perhaps most importantly, if you take your retirement funds as a single withdrawal, you may jeopardize your retirement.

So, what should you do?

Under the Internal Revenue Code (IRC) 72(t), you can withdraw funds from your IRA without penalty providing you follow certain guidelines.

As described under Section 72(t), a substantially equal series (SES) of payments can be an effective strategy for obtaining cash you need now while maintaining the savings that you may need later in retirement. Section 72(t) spells out the conditions under which a series of premature withdrawals can be made from an IRA without the usual tax penalty. It allows you to withdraw a stream of regular payments from your retirement savings, in accordance with certain rules, without incurring a 10% IRS penalty or the mandatory 20% withholding of taxes by your former employer. You will have to pay your regular income taxes on the distributions you receive. However, the bulk of your savings can continue to grow tax deferred. If taking 72(t) distributions is in your future, you must first roll over your retirement plan account into an IRA.

Any IRA owner may take an SES distribution at any time, for any reason. The size of your distribution will be based on your account balance and life expectancy.

Following are the current IRC 72(t) rules:

- You must receive a "substantially equal series of payments" on a regular basis no less than once a year. Any variation from the calculated distribution will result in a 10% penalty, plus interest, on your past distributions.

- You must use one of the three IRS-approved calculated methods such as life expectancy, amortization, or annuitization. While all three are based on your life expectancy or the joint life expectancy of you and a beneficiary, each produces a different figure.

- Keep in mind if you do take a 72(t) distribution, you must continue it for five years or until you reach age fifty-nine and a half, whichever is longer. Failing to do so will result in the 10% IRS early withdraw penalty along with interest on your past distributions.

Case Study: John Takes Early Retirement

John, a fifty-year-old employee forced to accept an early retirement, is eligible for a lump sum distribution of $300,000 from his 40l(k) plan. Not only is John uncertain about how long it will take to find a new job, he's not sure his new salary will be comparable to his previous one. What's more, he's facing a monthly cash flow shortage. John must generate an additional $750 per month to meet his monthly obligations. At the same time, John realizes that he needs to preserve his retirement savings for retirement while maintaining flexibility should his circumstances change.

Options:

1. Take the distribution in cash, pay current income taxes and penalties, and then invest the proceeds.

2. Directly roll over the $300,000 into an IRA.

3. Directly roll over only a portion of the $300,000, and pay income taxes and penalties on the balance. That portion would also be subject to the mandatory 20% federal income tax withholding.

4. Roll over to an IRA and take an SES distribution.

Considerations:

If John takes his distribution in cash, he'll lose his opportunity to invest the $135,000 due in taxes and penalties. With fifteen years left until retirement, this loss could be significant. Then again, if forced to tap his IRA account without the benefit of the 72(t) waiver, John will have to pay a 10% early withdraw penalty in addition to current income taxes on the amount he withdraws.

Goal: Generate cash flow of $750 per month.

Based on the counsel of his advisor, John:

- Splits the $300,000 distribution and establishes two IRAs of $150,000 each. He does this by doing a direct rollover and avoids the 20% withholding tax.

- Invests the first IRA in an income-oriented portfolio.

- Begins receiving monthly payments of $750 from the first IRA, using the annuitization calculation method based on a single life expectancy factor at an assumed interest rate of 7.5 percent.

- Invests the second IRA in a more growth-oriented portfolio which, based on a hypothetical 7% annual growth rate, would grow to almost $413,854 by the time he retires at age sixty-five.

- If John finds that he needs more than the $750 per month, SES payments can be started from his second IRA.

- If John finds another job and no longer needs the $750 per month, he can divert the income into another savings vehicle earmarked for retirement.

Outcome:

Even under IRC 72(t) strict rules, John was able to achieve, with the help of his financial advisor, his goals. If starting a 72(t) distribution is right for you, I'd encourage you to work with a financial advisor who is an expert in this area. Keep in mind that the IRS is rigid with regard to the amount of the payments and the payment.

Required Minimum Distributions (RMD)

When you reach age seventy and a half, you have to start taking withdrawals from your qualified retirement plans, including IRAs. (Roth IRAs do not require minimum withdrawals.) The key word here is "minimum." You can always take out more than the required minimum. The required minimum distribution for any year is the account balance as of the end of the previous year divided by a distribution period from the IRS's Uniform Lifetime Table. If the IRA owner's spouse is more than ten years younger, a separate table is used. Failure for not taking your RMD will result in a 50% excise tax on the amount not distributed as required. The IRS gives you until April 1st of the year following the year that you turn seventy and a half. The one problem with delaying your RMD is that you will be required to take an additional RMD for that year as well. We recommend taking your RMD in the same year that you turn age seventy and a half.

Chapter Six:

Making Money in the Capital Markets

Investing can be a frightening experience for many older Americans. All you have to do is think back to 2008. More than likely, at the end of 2007 millions of people were feeling pretty good about their retirement accounts and perhaps their chances for retiring early. The stock market meltdown left many looking like a deer caught in the headlights of a fast-approaching freight train.

A sound retirement plan requires a good understanding of basic investment strategies that will help you meet your short-term and long-term financial needs. While having a good understanding on how money is made and kept in the capital markets is probably on everyone's agenda, it's never been more difficult. According to a Dalbar study, investors consistently underperform the markets by some 60%. The reason? Investor behavior! Most of us invest without having any idea how investments work and, more importantly, have no idea how much risk we are incurring.

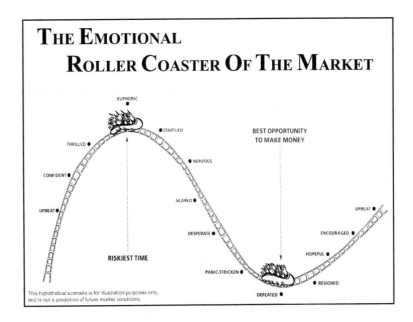

So where do the biggest mistakes occur? Is it when the market is reaching new highs and euphoria is replacing common sense, or is it when markets are in the tank and we're reeling with fear?

If you answered, "During both high and low periods," you'd be correct.

Often when markets are hitting new highs, it's easy to feel like everyone is making money except for you. So what do you do? If you're like most, you get more aggressive with your investments. Then what happens? The market goes down. It's Murphy's Law! Investments do really well until you invest in them and then, of course, they go down. The same holds true when markets are down for an extended period of time. We panic and move our money to the sidelines only to see the market take off shortly thereafter. Unless you learn from past mistakes, you're most likely to repeat past behavior until you go broke.

The securities market is one of the few areas that most people typically, and illogically, buy high. In contrast, when the securities are on sale after a decline, people tend to shy away from them. Crazy, isn't it? The best opportunities exist when the markets are down.

There are innumerable scenarios and situations when it comes to investing. My favorite rule of thumb is that there are no rules of thumb. The truth is that everyone's situation is unique and should be looked at individually.

Most people don't truly understand how money is made in the capital markets, and for this reason most people don't achieve good investment results. With 401(k) plans replacing many pensions, people are being forced to become investors.

I have found over the years that people are generally better savers than investors. It's important to understand that making more money than a bank account requires some level of risk. You can control some of the risk through diversification, but you can't eliminate it.

The market is a great mechanism to create wealth and income. At the same time the market is an extremely effective means to transfer wealth from the *impatient* to the *patient* investor. The following are my steps to help you to become a patient and successful investor.

Step 1. Don't panic!

Over the years, it has paid to stay invested during troubled times. We can learn a lot about investing by understanding the history of the market.

I was talking to a client last year during a market correction, and she told me that she was concerned about the market and her money. The fact that she was worried was understandable, and it's my job as an advisor to protect clients from their greatest risk, which is typically themselves. However, she said to me that at her age—sixty-four—she couldn't afford to gamble her life savings. I told her that I understood, and neither could I, for that matter; I'm not a gambler. In my entire life, I have not gambled more than twenty dollars.

I reminded her that the market odds are heavily in her favor. History tells us that over the past ninety years, the market has gone up three out of four years. At the beginning of every year there is a 75% chance that the market will be positive for that year. Not bad odds! However, history also tells us that during the same ninety years the market has averaged three 5% declines per year, one 10% decline every two years, and one 20% or greater decline every three and a half years. The average recovery time after a 20% correction or greater is twelve months. But the most important consideration is: after every market decline the market has recovered 100% of the time.

This chart shows what happened during the five-year period following major market declines:

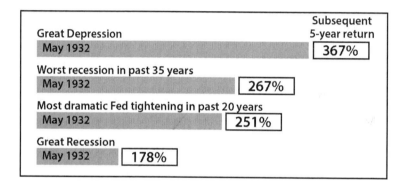

U.S. stock market returns represented by total return of S&P 500® Index. Past performance is no guarantee of future results. It is not possible to invest in an index.

First three dates determined by best five-year market return subsequent to the month shown, March 9, 2009–December 31, 2012. Sources: Ibbotson, Factset, FMRCo,

Asset Allocation Research Team as of December 31, 2013.

I don't know about you, but as long as you adhere to sound investing principles, I don't see investing as gambling. My recommendation is this: Don't concern yourself with bull and bear markets. They come and go, and there is not a thing you can do about it. Worrying about it gets you nowhere, except maybe an ulcer, or even worse, it can lead to making costly investment mistakes that could take years to recover from. I see market declines as *buying opportunities.* If wealth is going to transfer from the impatient to the patient, I'd rather be on the receiving end!

Before investing a single dollar, you need to implement an investment policy—an investment road map of sorts. This road map should take into consideration:

- Your age
- Time frame until the money will be needed
- What percentage of your retirement income will be dependent on these monies
- And perhaps most importantly, your comfort level with risk (One should never sacrifice a good night's sleep for financial reward!)

Step 2. Be comfortable with the potential best and worst-case scenarios.

I think it's important to know how much your investments can range and what you might experience. I believe that everyone is risk averse and would prefer a riskless return, but we all know that if you want to earn more than bank rates of return, you'll need some exposure to risk.

It's normal to be concerned about the ups and downs of the market, as long as you keep your cool during inevitable market downturns. I have seen clients become worried when the value of their portfolio dropped 5 percent. I can't help but think that we would all be better off if stocks were to be priced but once a year. Can you imagine if you received daily values of your home? If you did, would you sell your house if its value dropped 5%, or would you shrug it off because you knew that over the long haul real estate values go up?

If you believe that investing in the stock market is treacherous, or perhaps you've had a bad investment experience, it's easy to understand the fear that accompanies investing. I know because I was once fearful as well, until I became a student of the market and learned from investor greats like Warren Buffett. However, reality tells us that the stock market has been a highly reliable engine to creating wealth for long-term investors and a highly reliable way to losing wealth for short-term investors.

Before we go any further, let's define "investment risk." Investment risk to me means the odds of losing your investment. There is a vast difference between *risk* and *volatility*. I believe the only risk to investors who are properly diversified is the risk of selling due to panicking after the market has declined. By selling after a decline, you go from a *paper* loss (unrealized loss) to an *actual* loss. On the other hand, if you don't panic and sell, and the investment recovers, you haven't loss a thing. This describes volatility, or the variance between the highs and lows.

To give you an extreme example, if you owned stock that was priced at $50 per share on Monday, and on Tuesday it plunged to $10 per share, and then on Wednesday it was back up to $50 per share, should you have sold on Tuesday? Of course not! Yet this is exactly what happens over a period of months or even years. If you held a blue-chip stock portfolio in September of 2007, when the market was high, and didn't sell as the market tanked, by April 2012 you'd have been fully recovered and heading up in the bear market. Volatility? Yes. Risk to you? Very little.

If there were no risk or volatility, people would always gravitate to the highest yielding investments, and therefore lower yielding investments would cease to exist and everyone would get the same investment result and no one would aspire to a higher rate of return. As we all know, that isn't the real world. There is typically a correlation between returns and risk.

Risk is the primary concern of investors. Acceptance of risk is what separates our savings from investments. The successful investor must come to terms with the implications of accepting risk. One cannot hope for higher returns without accepting higher fluctuations.

Every investor must realize that there will be good days and there will be bad days. Bad days are built right into the investment strategy. Fortunately, history tells us that good days have outnumbered bad days three to one!

Please take some time to exam the chart below to fully understand how much your portfolio will deviate from peaks and valleys in any given period of time. As you can see, the higher the potential return, the greater the swings.

Know how much your portfolio will deviate—

PEAKS AND VALLEYS!

	Conservative	Balanced	Growth	Aggressive growth
U.S. stock Foreign stock Bond Short-term investments				
Annual return %				
Average	6.01	7.98	8.97	9.64
Best 12 months	31.06	76.57	109.55	136.07
Worst 12 months	-17.67	-40.64	-52.92	-60.78
Best 5 years	17.24	23.14	27.27	31.91
Worst 5 years	-0.37	-6.18	-10.43	-13.78

Data Source: Ibbotson Associates, 2014 (1926–2013). **Past performance is no guarantee of future results.** Returns include the reinvestment of dividends and other earnings. Associates 2014 (1926–2013).

Step 3. Consider the yield (dividends).

When I ask my valued clients how they make money in the stock market, I usually hear, "You make money when share prices go up." This is only partially true! How about dividends? Dividends give you a second way to make money, and dividends are much more predictable than share prices going up.

A dividend is the distribution of a company's earnings to their shareholders. I like to compare dividends to rentals. Most people that I know who invest in rentals do so primarily for the rental income.

The value of the property may go up in value over time, but who knows in the short term? It's a lot like the stock market.

One of the most frustrating aspects of owning shares in a company that doesn't pay dividends is that all profits are locked in your stock. The only way to access those profits is to sell shares. Companies who pay dividends allow you to take some profits without having to sell shares. Dividends allow you to receive profits even in a bear market.

Dividends become especially important when you are retired. Your retirement would be much more financially successful if you could live on dividends alone. You would avoid having to make money by selling more shares in a down market. Living on dividends alone may not be realistic these days; however, dividends should cover at least half, if not more, of your withdrawals.

As you may tell, I like dividends! With that said, I do not recommend simply seeking companies that are paying the highest dividends. It's important to know the company's overall financial health, including their P&L statement. A company that pays a dividend greater than their earnings is not sustainable, and will affect their share price.

Dividends are powerful even if you don't need the income because dividends can be used to purchase additional shares in the company. The easiest way to do this is through dividend reinvestment plans, most commonly known as DRIP.

Step 4. Consider liquidity!

For several reasons, it has always been my policy to never buy securities that are not publicly traded on a public exchange. First, the share prices are transparent and are current. Second, they can be sold immediately without having to find a buyer.

One of the most common non-traded securities is real estate investment trusts, or REITs. They can own brick and mortar properties, such as apartments, hotels, storage units, office buildings, and health care facilities, to name a few. They can also own debt, such as mortgages. The appeal of these investments are that typically the income they pay their shareholders is high. What people often don't realize is that a portion of the income they receive may include a return of principal.

Non-traded securities are illiquid, which means that they cannot be easily sold. Instead, investors generally must wait until the non-traded security goes public or is sold. There can be a secondary market, but it often requires the seller to sell their shares at a deep discount.

Fees on non-traded securities can be quite high. It's not unusual for these investments to carry up to a 15% sales charge along with high transaction costs and management fees.

I stay with investments that are registered with the SEC and are listed on the major exchanges. This means that these investments can be bought or sold easily. This also means that I know the value of the investment daily.

Step 5. Research your investments.

When I meet with prospective clients, I like to ask how they chose the investments that they own. What they tell me is interesting. I hear answers like, "I asked my coworker. He's always on the Internet looking at his 401(k) and he's always talking about the market, so

I figured he must know what he's doing, or at least he knows more about it than me."

Or, "My brother-in-law is always talking about how well he's doing, and he gets the *Wall Street Journal*, so I get my advice from him."

Or, "I pick whatever stocks did well last year."

This is not the way to build wealth! Whomever you may get advice from, it's important to know what qualifies them to give such critical advice.

I have studied the markets for many years, as well as some of the most successful investors of our time, and I can tell you that investing should never be willy-nilly. Following are the analytics I suggest when constructing a portfolio:

1. **Beta**—The measurement of risk compared to a benchmark. The benchmark that we typically use is the S&P 500. The benchmark will always have a Beta of 1.00, so if your investment or a portfolio has Beta of greater than 1.00, you can expect your risk to be *greater* than the S&P 500, while a Beta of less than 1.00 suggests *less* risk.

2. **Sharpe ratio**—Gives a risk-adjusted comparison. I find that folks often compare investments solely on returns without considering the risk-adjusted return. Case in point—when is an 8% return better than a 10% return? An 8% return is better when it is taken on 79% or less of the 10% investment.

3. **Standard deviation**—This is the dispersion of a set of data from its mean. With investments, standard deviation is applied to the annual rate of return of an investment to measure the

investment's volatility. A higher risk investment or more aggressive portfolio will have more volatility, and thus a higher standard deviation. This is important to know so that you have a good understanding how much your portfolio will deviate from its average return over a specified period of time. This will help avoid panic during a volatile period.

4. **Alpha**—Often considered the active return of an investment against a market index used as a benchmark. I like to think of it as how much added value an investment manager brings to their investors, either through better returns or reduced risk. Keep in mind that the investment should be in line with your tolerance to risk or beta that we discussed above.

5. **Expense Ratio**—The annual fee that all funds or ETFs charge their shareholders. This fee includes 12b-1 fees (distribution costs), management fees, administration fees, operating costs, and trading costs.

Index funds and ETFs want you to believe that you should choose an investment based on their fees alone; however, I believe that choosing investments with the lowest fees is shortsighted. While expenses are an important consideration, it shouldn't be your only consideration. Only after the first four analytics are considered should expenses come into play.

A lot of folks believe that index funds and ETFs are their best choice not only because of their low expenses but because their returns are hard to beat. It's been my experience that a portfolio that is primarily made up with actively managed funds with high alpha will often beat a portfolio made up of only index funds or ETFs.

There are a few problems to consider with index funds and ETFs. As you are probably aware, these investments are not actively managed, which will lead them to be overweighted in industries that have experienced greater growth than other sectors. Case in point, remember back in the 1990s when tech companies experienced crazy growth? By the end of the nineties, indexes like the S&P 500 became overweighted in tech, only to be whipsawed by the tech crash in 2000. It's been my observation that index funds and ETFs may do well in bull markets but carry much more volatility during bear markets.

So with all things being equal, your decision should be made based on returns net of expenses on a risk-adjusted basis.

Stay Diversified.

Regardless of where you invest, it's important to diversify among various asset classes. Many people's idea of diversification is having multiple mutual funds. Often I'll find that people who have multiple mutual funds are investing in many of the same securities. The problem with this type of allocation is that when one fund is down, they'll all be down. What an investor needs is securities that have *low correlation* with one another. On the other hand, government bonds have ranged from a positive 35% to a negative 10%, which is a much lower variance (standard deviation).

Diversification helps you achieve your investment goals by balancing risk and reward, although there is no guarantee that you will make a profit or that you will be protected from losses. Ideally, your portfolio should be invested in seven to eight sectors of the economy, such as financials, utilities, health care, technology, real estate, consumer goods, industrials, and telecommunications. In the late 1990s everyone seemed to be heavy in technology, and of course tech stocks took a dive after the turn of the century. The point is that you never know what the next "hot" sector is going to be, so keep your exposure diversified.

In addition to diversifying by sectors, you should diversify by *equity style*. Equity style can be divided into three areas—large, medium, and small capitalization ("cap") companies.

Each one of these areas can be broken down even further, beginning with value. *Value companies* often pay dividends and normally have less volatility than *growth companies*, which are using their earnings to grow their operations and market share. *Core companies* are companies that fall between growth and value. Even though our portfolios typically have a slightly heavier weighting in large cap value, we recommend having a percentage of your equities in all nine styles—large, medium, and small cap in value, growth, and core companies.

Fixed income or bonds play a major role in diversification. How much in bonds you have in your portfolio will depend greatly on your time horizon and your comfort level. When selecting bonds you'll want to consider their origin (corporate or government), grade (investment grade or noninvestment grade), maturity, and other associated risks such as interest rate risks and default risks.

Rebalance

If you want to prevent risk or volatility drift in your portfolio, you're going to want to periodically rebalance your portfolio. This is because asset classes will grow or decline at different rates, and even a conservative portfolio over time can become aggressive if not rebalanced.

Balance Risk and Return

When you diversify your investments across asset classes that perform differently in the same market conditions, you can potentially offset losses (risk) in one asset category with gains (reward) in another. This could lead to greater returns over time, but perhaps more importantly, it could reduce the chances of making bad allocation choices during extreme market volatility.

An asset allocation strategy doesn't guarantee against loss or guarantee a profit, but it certainly can improve your chances of success. If creating your own portfolio seems daunting, you may want to seek professional help.

Dos and Don'ts for Investors

What you should do:

✓ Invest with a purpose, keeping your financial goals in mind.

✓ Research investments and obtain sound financial advice before acting.

✓ Stay diversified, and don't chase short-term returns!

✓ If you work with an investment advisor, make sure that they are registered with the SEC as a Registered Investment Advisor (RIA).

An RIA has a fiduciary responsibility to their clients. An RIA should always put the interest of their client ahead of theirs. You should always check out the advisor at SEC.gov to make sure they meet your requirements and that they have a clean record. You can never learn too much about a person whom you're going to entrust to manage your wealth.

✓ Avoid any investments or promoters of schemes promising unusually high returns with no or little risk. Over the years I have found that these types of investments usually go south.

✓ Avoid investments that are marketed by phone. The Federal Trade Commission says about three quarters of fraudulent investment schemes are pitched over the phone.

✓ Report unscrupulous sales people to FINRA.org or SEC.gov.

✓ Make sure you understand your risk tolerance. During a huge market decline, you don't want to discover that you are more risk averse than you thought. Ask yourself at what point you would abandon your long-term investment plan and run to the comforts of cash. Is it after a 10% decline? Maybe it's 20%, 30%, or even a 50% decline. Be honest with yourself when it comes to your risk tolerance, and make sure that your investment portfolio matches your comfort level.

✓ Embrace volatility as your best friend. Market declines offer opportunities to buy low. Remember that the market has always recovered from declines!

What you *shouldn't* do:

- Don't think you can retire on a lump sum of money. You retire on the *income* the lump sum generates.

- Don't invest in investments that you don't understand, even if a friend recommends them.

- Don't put all of your eggs in one basket. Diversify! Don't assume more risk than you can tolerate. I know I covered this in the "what to dos" above, but it's worth repeating.

- Don't buy an investment that isn't publicly traded. A nonliquid investment spells S-P-E-C-U-L-A-T-I-V-E to me, and I have always steered away from these types of investments.

- Don't let tax incentives drive your investment decisions. Tax laws are subject to change. Your number-one investment consideration should be determining if the proposed action fits into your long-term objectives.

- Don't use long-term investments to solve short-term financial needs. Other than for income purposes, I never invest in securities of any kind to reach a goal in fewer than five years.

- Don't choose investments solely on returns. Always consider the Sharpe ratio or the risk-adjusted return.

- Never make a check payable to an advisor for investment purposes. I think it's a good idea to work with a firm that is not also the custodian of your investments. Separation is a good idea.

To wrap up this chapter, I want to remind you that probably the greatest investment risk you're going to face is *you!* The more you understand how money is made in the capital markets, the better off you'll be. If you also understand the psychology behind making money, the odds of making money are in your favor.

Chapter Seven:

A Penny Saved Is a Penny Earned: Tax Planning

Over two hundred years ago, one of our most distinguished and accomplished founding fathers made an astute and profound observation on the issue of taxation: "In this world," Benjamin Franklin said, "nothing can be said to be certain except death and taxes."

It is true that many older taxpayers—about half, according to the IRS—pay little if any income tax. This is because they have little if any income and have saved little for retirement. However, since you are reading this book, you are most likely among the majority who have lived below their means and have worked extremely hard to save for their retirement. What this means is that you have, and probably still are, paying plenty in taxes, regardless if you are still working or are already retired.

Taxes may be your greatest single expense. On average, Americans work 111 days to pay their taxes, which includes federal, state, and local taxes. I believe one of the most important things you can do to bolster your retirement and to achieve financial independence is to learn how to keep more of what you earn.

It can be a challenge to accumulate enough assets for retirement when taxes take a significant chunk of your take-home pay. How can you get the greatest tax savings from your itemized deductions? How can you get the biggest tax savings through employee benefit programs? These are all issues that most of us face every year. In this chapter we will examine various strategies that you can implement yourself immediately and that can save you thousands of dollars.

The following tax tips are general in nature and should be tailored to your specific situation. If you think any of these ideas make sense to you, I encourage you to discuss them with your tax advisor.

Tax Tips

Tax Tip #1: Make sure it makes sense.
The first important lesson of tax savings is that no matter how much a strategy might save you in taxes, it ultimately has to make sense and fit into your financial goals and objectives. I have seen folks do foolish things in order to save taxes with little regard to whether or not they make financial sense. So don't become penny wise only to be pound foolish.

Tax Tip #2: Minimize your taxable income.

Deferring tax liability makes sense for two reasons: Most individuals are in a higher tax bracket in their *working years* than their *retirement years*. So deferring income until retirement will most likely result in paying fewer taxes in retirement. Additionally, by using the tax deferral of a retirement account, you not only save taxes today, but you get to invest the money that you would have otherwise paid in taxes.

Many employers offer retirement plans, such as a 401(k), or a 403(b) for those who work for nonprofit organizations, where an employee can elect to defer a portion of his salary. As of 2017, an employee can defer up to $18,000, plus an additional $6,000 catch-up if the employee is age fifty and over. (For current limits, visit www.irs.gov.) You'll need to check with your employer to see how much their plan allows.

Some employers match a portion of the employee's contribution, which makes participating in such a plan even sweeter. Even if your employer doesn't do any matching, I still believe you should contribute as much as you can because not only will it save you taxes, but it will help you save for retirement, too.

If you have your own business—even if your business is less than full time—numerous types of plans are available for you to set up. Plans range from the simplest of plans such as the Simple IRAs to defined benefit plans. If you're considering a plan for your business, it would be wise to sit down with a qualified advisor to determine which plan may be right for you.

Tax Tip #3: Take advantage of tax-deductible retirement plans.
If you work for an employer that does not offer a retirement plan, you are eligible to take a full deduction for an IRA contribution. The current maximum contribution limit is $5,500 and a $1,000 catch-up provision if the person is fifty or older. Again, you can find out current limits by visiting the IRS web site at www.irs.gov. If you have a spouse, you can make a tax-deductible contribution to a Spousal IRA even if you are covered by an employer plan or if your spouse has little or no earned income, providing your AGI is less than $184,000 for the tax year.

Tax Tip #4: Look for tax-deferred investment accounts.
Once you have taken full advantage of pretax and tax deductible investments, consider looking for tax-deferred accounts. If your AGI is less than $184,000 for married couples filing jointly, or $117,000 for singles, you may want to consider contributing to a Roth IRA. Your contributions are nondeductible; however, the money grows tax deferred, and withdrawals are tax free if held for five years or age fifty-nine and a half, whichever is the greater of the two. Your contribution limits are the same as an IRA.

Another tax-deferred plan uses annuities. Regardless of your tax bracket or income level, your money in an annuity is free of taxes until you start making withdrawals. Keep in mind that your original investment will not be taxed, which can lead to lower taxes when you start making withdrawals, either by annuitizing the contract or by making systematic withdrawals. Please note that withdrawals prior to age fifty-nine and a half may be subject to a 10% federal penalty tax.

Tax Tip #5: Defer bonuses or other earned income.
If you are due a bonus at year-end, check with your employer to see if you can defer receipt of these funds until January. This would defer taxes for another year. If you're self-employed, you can consider waiting to send out invoices until after the next year begins. This is particularly good if you're going to be in a lower tax bracket in the following year.

Tax Tip #6: Accelerate capital losses and defer capital gains.
If you have investments that you have incurred losses on, it may be advantageous to sell them prior to year-end. You can deduct capital losses up to the amount of your capital gains.

If you don't have any gains to offset your losses, you can still take a $3,000 deduction each year until you have used up your losses. If you are selling an investment that has a gain, it may be best to wait until after the end of the year, which would defer taxes until the following year. You may want to wait to sell your taxable investment until you have held it for more than twelve months. This way you would incur capital gains tax rates rather than incurring ordinary income tax rates. Currently, the maximum capital gains rate is 20 percent.

What if the stock that has gone down has promised to rebound? You can sell it to create a loss and repurchase it after thirty days.

It goes without saying that you should make sure to consider the economic value of the investment. Don't sell something strictly for tax purposes.

Tax Tip #7: Contribute to a Health Savings Account (HSA).
An HSA is a tax-advantaged medical savings account you can contribute to and draw money from for certain medical expenses tax free, providing you are enrolled in a high-deductible health plan. Your contributions are not subject to federal income tax at the time of deposit and can be withdrawn to pay qualified health care expenses. Currently an HAS can be paired with any plan with an annual deductible of more than $1,300 for a single person and $2,600 for family coverage. Annual contribution limits are $3,350 for an individual and $6,650 for a family. Persons aged fifty-five and older can contribute an extra $1,000.There is no "use it or lose it" clause like Flex Spending Accounts.

Tax Tip #8: Be charitable minded.
If you're planning to make a charitable gift, it generally makes more sense to give appreciated assets to the charity. If you sell the asset first, you'll owe taxes and have less to give to the charity. If the charity sells the appreciated asset, the organization will not owe any taxes. Additionally, you can obtain a tax deduction for the fair market value of the property. In some cases it may make sense to give depreciated assets to a charity as well. The deduction will be based on fair market value, which may actually be more than you can get by selling the gift outright. Don't forget to file an information return on contributions of $501 to $5,000. Except for publicly traded securities, if the gift exceeds $5,000 you will need a qualified appraisal.

Whether you are donating an asset or cash, you may want to consider whether the charity offers any type of credits. A tax credit offers a dollar-for-dollar reeducation in your tax liability. I address this in more detail under tax tip #11.

You'll want to make sure the charity is qualified by the IRS so that you can deduct your donations. Generally, houses of worship, most nonprofit charities, and education organizations such as schools and museums are qualified. You may want to check out the following websites for additional information:

Give.org—The site, run by the Better Business Bureau Wise Giving Alliance, offers tips and free reports on national charities.

Guidestar.org—A database of nonprofits that allows you to search for a nonprofit and do research on charities before you give them money.

Charitywatch.org—Site of the American Institute of Philanthropy, a charity watchdog service.

If in doubt, you can write to the charity and ask them to send you a copy of their IRS *letter of determination*, which is the best evidence that a charity is authorized to accept tax-deductible donations.

Tax Tip #9: Keep track of mileage driven for business, medical, or charitable purposes.

If you drive your car for business, medical, or charitable purposes, you may be entitled to deduct the miles driven. Beginning January 1, 2017, the standard mileage rates are:

- 53.5 cents per mile for business miles driven
- 17 cents per mile driven for medical or moving purposes
- 14 cents per mile driven in service of charitable organizations

You need to keep detailed daily records of the mileage driven for each of these purposes in order to substantiate the deductions.

Tax Tip #10: Set up a home equity loan or a line of credit.
If you have consumer-related interest expenses, such as interest from car loans and credit cards or any other nondeductible interest expenses, you may want to consider setting up a home equity loan or a home equity line of credit. Interest from either one of these types of loans is typically tax deductible. Make sure that the net cost (after the tax savings) of the loan is less than what you may be already paying on the nondeductible loan.

Tax Tip #11: Take advantage of tax credits.
Rarely do I see folks taking advantage of tax credits. Most of us are familiar with items that are *tax deductions*, such as mortgage interest or contributions into a tax-deductible IRA. These items will lower the amount of taxes due based on your tax bracket. For instance, if you have $1,000 as a deduction and you're in a 35% tax bracket, you save $350 in taxes.

Tax credits are quite different. Tax credits are a dollar-for-dollar reduction of your taxes. So, if you have $1,000 in tax credits you save $1,000 in taxes. Do I have your attention? I thought so.

The IRS offers a wide range of tax credits. They include earned income tax credit, mortgage interest credit, adoption credit, health coverage tax credit, credit for the elderly or disabled, foreign tax credit, and many more.

For example, low-income housing tax credits are issued by the U.S. Treasury Department for the purpose of providing affordable housing for Americans of moderate means. What this means is that if you invest in qualified housing or in a company that builds and manages properties that house folks who meet the government's definition of modest means, you would be eligible to receive these tax credits.

Congress budgets and awards each property's entire tax credit amount up front. The tax credit is generated when properties are rented to eligible tenants. Unlike most investments, tax credits are allocated at a predetermined rate and don't vary with changes in interest rates or fluctuations in the stock or bond markets.

In addition to benefiting you, the investor, by lowering your taxes dollar for dollar, the residents benefit as well. The elderly, handicapped, and working families with moderate incomes benefit by living in quality housing at affordable rents. Low-income housing tax credits are fully defined in Internal Revenue Code, Section 42 (they're often called "Section 42 credits).

Tax Tip #12: Watch out for stealth taxes.
Politicians don't want to increase taxes because it doesn't help them to get reelected, so instead they sneak in a bunch of what I call "stealth taxes." Some examples of these include increased taxes on dividends and capital gains, Medicare premium surtaxes, reduction in itemized deductions, and more. These days, it's rare for someone's taxes and tax rates to decline after retiring. As an example, in 1993 100% of Social Security benefits used to be tax free, but now, if a couple earns more than $44,000, 85% of their benefits are subject to a 3.8%

Medicare surtax for couples who earn too much. In 2017, the 7.5% of AGI floor for deducting medical expenses jumped to 10 percent. Currently, dividends and long-term capital gains are taxed at 20% instead of 15% for higher incomers, and the list goes on.

Reducing the amount of your hard-earned money that you give to the government is one of those things that you can do yourself, and you can do it immediately. I think you would agree that saving a thousand dollars or more every year in taxes could make a big difference, both in your current financial situation and in your retirement plans. While I am a strong advocate of paying your fair share, and I know that taxes are a necessity to pay for many of the things that make this country great, I do believe that finding legal ways to reduce your tax burden is not only a fundamental American right but a fundamentally American characteristic as well. After all, the tax issue was perhaps a driving force behind the creation of this great nation in the first place.

Chapter Eight:

A Purposeful Retirement

One hundred and fifty years ago, there was no such thing as retirement. With the Industrial Revolution still in its infancy, the vast majority of human beings lived on farms, where the rule was simple: You worked until you dropped dead. If you were too old to work in the fields, you did chores around the house. Even if you were infirm, you were likely to engage in some sort of value-creating activity, like knitting or helping in the kitchen.

By 1881, the attitude toward a lifetime of work was beginning to change. In that year, Otto von Bismarck, the president of Prussia, proposed the world's first plan for government-run financial support for older members of society. He argued to the Reichstag, "Those who are disabled from work by age and invalidity have a well-grounded claim to care from the state." Eight years later, the German government created the first government-sponsored retirement system, which provided for citizens over the age of seventy, if they lived that long.

As the developed nations shifted to heavy industry and more people left their farms to work in cities, it became obvious that as industrial workers got older they needed to be taken off the factory floor and retired.

Fast forward to the postwar era in the United States. The common template for an industrial or business worker became: Work for a paycheck until you're sixty-five, retire from work, and then either move to Florida and play golf or stay at home and help with the grandchildren. You'd putter around until you couldn't care for yourself, at which point you'd check into a rest home and play bridge or shuffleboard with the other inmates until you died.

Retirement was a reward. For forty years you had slaved away in the rat race, and in your golden years you deserved to kick back and enjoy the fruits of your labor.

You don't need me to tell you those days are over. Longer life spans, fewer body-punishing industrial jobs, and higher expectations have created a richer and more complex definition of retirement.

The fact is that many seniors *like* to work and *want* to work. They reach sixty-five and think, "I don't feel any different than when I was forty. I'm not going to just sit around and do nothing for the next twenty years. I want to stay active!"

This desire to stay engaged—to keep *living*—is tempered by the reality that even if they keep working, most seniors aren't going to be making the same income as they did in their prime. With less cash coming in, if they want to maintain a comfortable lifestyle they'll need to have built a significant nest egg from which to draw.

The other chapters in this book are all about that nest egg, and the important tasks of creating it and preserving it.

This chapter isn't about the money. It's about all the other things that can make your retirement fulfilling and productive. It's important to be both financially and *emotionally* ready to retire. This means that you don't grab your gold watch, go home, and then try to figure out what you want to do for the next twenty or thirty years. You need to plan ahead.

Baby boomers who are approaching retirement are searching for more meaningful lives; and more than their parents before them, they are now contemplating personal identity, life meaning, and core values. While with the help of qualified financial planners new retirees can develop a clear game plan for navigating the financial territory of retirement, the new terrain of life itself may be unfamiliar.

Just as they need a map for financial planning, they'd like a map for life planning, too.

An Unfamiliar Sense of Freedom

As you transition from your working life into retirement, you need to prepare for an adjustment period and a time of transition. Like any other life transition, this transition includes letting go of the past and creating a new path in your life. Retirement changes not only daily routines, but it may also change what is important to you, your relationships, your sense of who you are, and how you find some sense of value in the world.

Let's talk about your schedule. You may very well have spent, or will spend, forty years getting up at the crack of dawn and commuting to your job, returning home after dark. In retirement, if you choose not to work, your day will no longer be ruled by the stern demands of the clock. Your calendar will no longer be filled with work obligations. Some people embrace this new freedom. For many others—perhaps for you—it's uncomfortable. The freedom to choose without external constraints for the first time in one's life can be scary and daunting. There's nothing wrong with this, and in fact having regular habits can lead to less stress and a freedom of a different sort.

Here's the point: In your so-called retirement, you should be able to do *whatever you want as long as it's legal and you can afford it!* It's as simple as that.

If going to work every day is what you want, then that's exactly what you should do. (In the pages ahead I'll introduce you to some folks who, at the age of ninety and even one hundred, have chosen to get up, get out, and go to work every day—and they love it.)

It's likely that retirement is the first time in your life when you have the opportunity to make deliberate and meaningful choices regarding how you want to spend your time and energy, without following an externally dictated structure created by work or family roles, such as being a mother who needs to pick up a child every day at school and take her to ballet class. (One of the benefits of being a grandparent is that such duties are most often elective, not mandatory.)

So how will you choose to spend your time? And will the way in which you choose to spend your time truly reflect who you are and what you value most in your life? Will you choose to keep working in some capacity, or buy a boat and island-hop around the Caribbean?

As you recalibrate, think about how your priorities may shift and how your values may evolve. Does your present plan—if you have one—accurately reflect what you want out of your life? Here are some key questions to ask yourself to determine whether your newly charted course in retirement reflects who you want to be and what you truly want out of your life.

What are your options? The first thing you need to do is take stock of your finances. Wanting to buy a yacht and sail around the world may be a nice dream, but it may not be feasible. On the other hand, rafting down the Colorado River through the Grand Canyon may be both rewarding and within reach. In the pages ahead you'll see lots of ideas for retirement activities that are surprisingly affordable.

What is truly important to you? Do you have to keep earning money to maintain your lifestyle, or can you downsize and have more freedom? If money were no object, what would become your passion? Do you have a current hobby that you can expand or even monetize?

Do you have existing responsibilities—and how do you feel about them? Many people entering retirement are caring for an aging parent, which takes up time and energy. You may have other family obligations that you can't walk away from. On the other hand, you may want to take on *new* responsibilities, such as joining the board of the local art museum or volunteering at the food bank.

At Townsend Retirement, we encourage you to openly discuss—with your spouse, family, and advisors—the important areas of your life that will impact your retirement and how you live it. We call them the Five Life Centers, which feed and nurture you as you step into this new exciting phase.

1. Purpose

Your purpose is the activity that gets you up in the morning and sustains you. It's the thing or things you most look forward to. It may be an extension of your previous work, or it may be something entirely new.

Here's a fascinating example.

The name George W. Bush is familiar to everyone. He was the forty-third president of the United States. On January 20, 2009, he retired from his job. He was sixty-three years old. For several years after retirement, he kept a low profile, and few people knew what he was doing with his time. But eventually word got out that President Bush had taken up painting. It was something he had never done before. Most people thought, "Isn't that nice—he has a new hobby." But in March 2017 he published a book entitled *Portraits of Courage*, showcasing sixty-six of his portraits of military personnel and veterans. Guess what? It hit the bestseller lists and revealed that the president had become a serious artist. These were no amateur doodles; his work was truly outstanding and was taken seriously by people in the art community. It's possible that if he continues painting, George W.

Bush may become known as the famous artist who also happened to once have been a president.

If you're not an artist, working or volunteering in the area of your interest may be a perfect vehicle for finding your life purpose. Many retirees work part time. They work for:

1. Purpose and fulfillment—they want to make the world a better place
2. Self-esteem—they want to feel valued
3. Companionship and a sense of community—they don't want to be lonely
4. Extra cash

In other words, while the financial component—the cash—may not be at the top of the list, many seniors keep working for the same reasons that other people work. It's because most human beings don't like sitting around all day. It's not in our nature. We like to do stuff!

Take Sara Dappen. As reported by the *New York Daily News* in 2013, Sara Dappen, then age ninety-two, was the oldest known McDonald's employee in the world. She had been at the Story City, Iowa, location for five years.

Born in 1920, she could be found most days flipping burgers. Dappen said her favorite part of the job was chatting with visitors. "I thought it was more interesting to keep walking around here than to be walking up and down the street, and this keeps me from sitting," she told Oklahoma City's KOCO.com.

McDonald's department manager Elizabeth Holmes commented, "I think it's crazy, and she's going to be like one hundred and ten and working at McDonald's."

It's not just Dappen who benefitted—colleagues said that her life experience helped other workers, who said they felt inspired by how she handled herself.

If fast food isn't for you, consider the story of Irving Kahn. Born December 19, 1905, until his death on February 24, 2015, at the age of 109, Kahn was the oldest living active Wall Street investor. Chairman of Kahn Brothers Group, Inc., a privately owned investment advisory and broker-dealer firm, he began his career in 1928 and continued to work until the end. Since he owned the company, he didn't have to worry about a mandatory retirement age. In a magazine article in 2002, he was quoted as saying: "I'm at the stage in life where I get a lot of pleasure out of finding a cheap stock," and his enthusiasm for his career pushed him to work evenings and weekends. As the *New York Times* reported, until he died Kahn continued to scour newspapers and magazines. In his last hours, his grandson Andrew, a research analyst at his grandfather's firm, had been reading an *Economist* cover article to him on the subject of Vladimir Putin.

2. Recreation

All work and no play make Jack a dull boy—and that goes for Jill, too! As with their attitude toward work, in wanting to have fun, seniors are no different from anybody else. Gone are the days when seniors were expected to play bridge and shuffleboard all afternoon until eating dinner at five in the afternoon. Nowadays, nothing is off limits as long as you're physically able.

Because of better health, seniors are doing things that are quite adventurous. For example, the father of artist George W. Bush, George H. W. Bush, also a former president, spent his ninetieth birthday plummeting to earth from thousands of feet in the air. Just as he did for birthdays eighty and eighty-five, Bush 41 marked the end of his ninth decade with a parachute jump. Aided by an ex-military jumper, Bush made the leap near his home in Kennebunkport, Maine. Of course, parachuting was nothing new to him—his first parachute jump took place when his fighter plane was shot down over the Pacific island of Chi Chi Jima on September 2, 1944.

Here are some activities that many of our clients pursue—perhaps one of them is right for you.

Hiking

It's long been known that to live a longer healthier life, staying in motion is important. For adults, regular aerobic exercise, including hiking, leads to improved cardio-respiratory fitness, lower risk of high blood pressure and type 2 diabetes, better muscular fitness, lower risk of coronary heart disease and stroke, and many more benefits.

Sitting on the sofa isn't what most retirees want to do anymore because it's boring and doesn't help you stay fit. Taking a nice long stroll could mean something as simple as going out your front door and walking around the block or to the park. But why not take your walking game to the next level and find spectacular places to hike? In

the United States we have some of the most amazing national parks
in the world, including these hiking hot spots:

- The Great Smoky Mountains National Park, featuring eight
  hundred miles of hiking trails across North Carolina and
  Tennessee. You can drive into the park on its 384 miles of
  mountain roads, pull off the road, park your car, and hike one
  of Great Smoky's many Quiet Walkways.

- Yosemite National Park in California, about which John Muir
  wrote, "No temple made with human hands can compete with
  Yosemite." Most of the five million annual visitors hike around
  the Yosemite Valley, the mile-wide, seven-mile-long canyon
  cut by a river and then widened and deepened by glacial action.
  Novice hikers will especially enjoy the guided tours and climbing
  lessons available from local adventure outfitters.

- Rocky Mountain National Park in Colorado, whose main
  attractions are the sweeping vistas. The park contains 450
  miles of streams and 150 lakes, plus ecosystems ranging from
  pine forests and wetlands to alpine tundra. It's only a two-hour
  drive from Denver, and visitors enter through Trail Ridge Road,
  traversing a spectacular ridge above 11,000 feet for ten miles.
  The dozens of hiking routes are rated according to difficulty,
  from the easy Lily Lake Loop to the challenging Longs Peak,
  which at 14,259 feet is the highest point in the park.

- Glacier National Park in northwestern Montana offers more
  than 700 miles of breathtaking hiking trails. Known to Native
  Americans as the "Backbone of the World," the park encompass-
  es more than one million acres of some of the most spectacular

scenery on earth. This national park is full of wildlife—while taking in the scenery of pristine mountains and fresh water streams, you may catch a glimpse of elk, mountain goats, or even grizzly bears (just don't feed them!).

- Acadia National Park in Maine offers over 120 miles of verdant forest trails and rugged coastal paths. They're often interconnected and range in difficulty from easy to strenuous. The Carriage Roads and stone bridges in Acadia are ideal for hikers, bikers, horseback riders, and—yes—carriages. If you hike along the water, keep your eyes open for harbor seals sunning themselves on granite outcroppings as peregrine falcons circle high in the sky.

- Olympic National Park in Washington State offers hikers three distinct ecosystems: subalpine forest and wildflower meadow, temperate forest, and the rugged Pacific shore. While no road traverses the park, several spur roads lead into it from US 101, providing access from outside the park. Hiking is a great way to explore the Olympic Peninsula, and you can either choose self-guided hikes or guided hikes from Lake Crescent Lodge.

Snowshoeing

Hiking is considered a fair-weather activity. So how do retirees stay active in the winter? Of course, skiing is popular, and if you're a skier you probably already know your favorite resort, whether it be Telluride, Vail, Aspen, or even somewhere in Europe like the French Alps. But if you're looking for something more like hiking, how about snowshoeing? Anyone who hikes can quickly master snowshoeing, and grandparents and parents alike find it an enjoyable activity to share with children and grandchildren.

Obviously, to go snowshoeing you need plenty of snow, so you have to either head north or into the mountains. One of the most popular snowshoeing destinations is Rocky Mountain National Park. A family friendly activity that's open to all skill levels, snowshoeing is a great way to explore the park's trails. Beginners or those new to the park may wish to take advantage of guided snowshoe treks.

Like hiking in the summer, before starting your journey you need to be prepared. Especially around the town of Estes Park, which is the gateway to the Rocky Mountain National Park, a popular snowshoeing time is January through March, when the weather can change quickly. You'll be ready if you wear warm and waterproof boots, dress in layers, and bring plenty of water and healthy snacks. When snowshoeing through deep snow, it's best to use ski poles or instep crampons to help you make your way. And you'll need a map, because many trails look unfamiliar when they're covered in snow.

Of course, Rocky Mountain National Park isn't the only place you can enjoy snowshoeing. All across America—at least where's there's snow—state and national parks offer opportunities for winter hiking. In New York State you can visit Black Rock State Forest, and Utah offers the Wasatch Range. At Mt. Rainier National Park in Washington State, you can experience the drama of a mountainside winter on snowshoes. There are plenty of snowshoe trails; for example, the Goat Falls Trail is a short snowshoe trip to a picturesque waterfall tucked away in a hidden rocky slot. Except for one small spot, it's an easy trek on snowshoes and ideal for beginners.

In state parks in Wisconsin, Minnesota, New Hampshire, and many other states you can even snowshoe by candlelight! The park sets out candles in paper bags or even in ice sculptures to gently light your way. Even if you've been married to the same person for thirty or forty years, a snowshoe hike by candlelight is sure to awaken romance. Even better, many programs offer cozy fires and warm beverages at the end of the trail.

Hunting and Shooting

In the United States, hunting is a big business. According to the U.S. Fish and Wildlife Service, roughly 12.5 million Americans spend nearly $30 billion each year on hunting activities and supplies. Many state legislatures have enacted legislation to afford senior citizens, veterans, and active duty military members special hunting and fishing opportunities and discounted fees. For example, the State of Kentucky offers "a senior lifetime combination hunting and fishing license, which remains valid until the death of the holder and authorizes the holder to perform all acts valid under a sport fishing license, a sport hunting license, and a state permit to take deer, turkey, trout, waterfowl, and migratory shore and upland game birds."

There's absolutely no reason why your retirement should mean forgoing the activities you've pursued or the dreams you've had; in fact, retirement can be the best time to make them come true. Hunting is a sport that you can keep doing well into retirement, and in fact some of the best hunters are senior citizens. Rocky Mountain National Park in Colorado, where the hunting season starts at the beginning of September and continues until late December, has great opportunities for elk, mule deer, and antelope hunting. A wide variety of big game outfitting and guide services are available in Colorado for big game hunters and bow hunters on non-guided big-game excursions and drop camps on private Colorado ranches.

Many retirees want to go further afield, to the big-game preserves in Africa. A big-game African hunting safari can be an exhilarating experience. Regardless of whether it's a one-time trip of a lifetime or just the beginning of many visits to this ancient and mysterious land, a big-game hunting safari can create unforgettable memories.

Typically, hunters are stalking the "big five": the African lion, African elephant, Cape buffalo, African leopard, and rhinoceros. The term "big five game" refers to the five most difficult animals in Africa to hunt on foot. They are among the most dangerous and yet most popular species for big-game hunters to hunt. Countries where all the members of the big five can be found include Botswana, Zambia, Uganda, Namibia, Ethiopia, South Africa, Kenya, Tanzania, Zimbabwe, the Democratic Republic of the Congo, and Malawi.

Planning your big-game African hunting safari requires a bit of homework. The key decision is your choice of outfitter, who can "make or break" your safari experience. You need to make sure the guides are members of the professional hunter's association for the country that you intend to visit, and they must be experienced in taking the species of game that you are interested in hunting. They should be able to provide references.

When you embark on your hunting trip, do you want to travel in style or "rough it?" Many retirees who travel to Africa seek to combine their hunting safari with a stay at a luxurious lodge. This is often the case when a hunter is traveling with his family (most hunters are men, but this is changing), and he wants to provide a luxury holiday and entertaining activities for his wife or family while he's out shooting at animals. Safari resorts can be incredibly luxurious. After a day of lion and elephant shooting—with gun or camera—your resort's amenities might include private chefs, private infinity pools, personal butlers, rangers and trackers, lounges, libraries, a spa with a "healing journey" treatment involving semiprecious jewels, and spacious decking areas rigged out with pillow-stuffed settees. You might get your own enormous tent, complete with working fireplace and full bar, and meals on your tent's private deck, with a telescope and bottles of vintage wine to make the day more pleasant.

If shooting a gun or crossbow at animals isn't your thing, you might enjoy shooting at clay pigeons or targets. There are three "shotgun sports" or major disciplines of competitive and recreational shooting: trapshooting, skeet shooting, and sporting clays. In each case the target is a clay disc, like a small Frisbee, that's launched into the air. The targets are often called clay pigeons.

In trap shooting, the clay pigeons are launched from a single "house" or machine, generally in a direction away from the shooter. In skeet shooting, clay pigeons are launched from two houses on opposite sides of the shooter, and paths of the targets intersect in front of the shooter.

Sporting clays involves a more complex course, with many launch points.

Now practiced all over the world, trapshooting was originally developed to provide a method of practice for bird hunters. It's been a sport since the late eighteenth century when real birds were used—usually passenger pigeons, which were extremely abundant at the time. Birds were placed under hats or in traps and then released. The first mechanical trap machine used to launch clay targets was introduced in 1909, and over the years, the use of targets grew as a replacement for the live pigeons; hence the name "clay pigeon." The idea was to mimic the behavior of the game birds as they were flushed out of the tall grass by the hunting dogs.

Increasingly, the word "shooting" refers not to guns but cameras. Photographic safaris and tours can be a rewarding experience for both husband and wife. Recent years have seen an increase in photographic safaris as well as tours of regional highlights. One interesting thing about photo safaris is that your "shooting" need not be confined to animals. For example, your safari to Tanzania might include visiting a school followed by observing a local initiation ritual, where you learn about the culture from the village chief and his family. You can document the daily life of the people and capture the spirit of traditional song and dance. Then you might descend to the base of the Ngorongoro Crater—the world's largest inactive, intact, and unfilled volcanic caldera—whose volcanic slopes shelter an abundance of animals. You can test your wildlife photography skills on rhinos, elephants, cheetahs, and other big game; record the interactions of prey and predator; and zoom in on avian species from rainbow-hued lovebirds to marabou storks.

Of course, you need not go to Africa to capture amazing scenes with your camera. Countless areas of the United States, from the majestic Rocky Mountains to the lava fields of Hawaii, offer spectacular opportunities for shutterbugs to make new memories.

3. Community Connection

Human beings are social creatures. It's a scientific fact that most people who live to a ripe old age generally have a solid network of friends and colleagues with whom they share life experiences, and to whom they can turn for support. In fact, studies have shown that the single most powerful predictor of life satisfaction after retirement is not always health or wealth, but the size of one's social network. Loneliness and isolation can be more detrimental to good health than bad habits such as smoking or not exercising.

As you and your partner plan for retirement, staying plugged into your community—or building relationships in a new community—is an important consideration. One option, of course, is to simply stay where you are and keep doing the same things you've always done, like going to the same church or belonging to the same clubs. There's nothing wrong with that, and many people who live long and fulfilling lives don't make any big changes as they get older.

Here are some community activities that are popular with retirees that may be either familiar or new to you.

RV Camping

Will you be driving down the road to retirement in a luxury recreational vehicle or motor home? While camping has been around for centuries, the idea of taking your home on the road began in the early twentieth century. "The first motorized campers were built in 1910," David Woodworth, a preeminent collector of early recreational vehicles and RV camping memorabilia, told GoRVing.com. "Before then, people camped in private rail cars that were pulled to sidings along train routes. The year 1910 brought a new freedom to people who didn't want to be limited by the rail system. RVs allowed them to go where they wanted, when they wanted." In that year, the first camping trailers were introduced by Los Angeles Trailer Works and Auto-Kamp Trailers, while the Pierce-Arrow "Touring Landau," a self-contained camper complete with an onboard bathroom, made its debut at Madison Square Garden. The period from 1910–1930 saw an explosion of interest in RVing. People wanted to be on the move and experience the country in a new way, and thousands of camping clubs were established across the country. As people loaded up their new vehicles to traverse the nation, the first "road trips" came into existence.

The archetypal RV trailer is the Airstream. The company was created by Wally Byam, a Los Angeles lawyer, during the late 1920s. In 1936, he introduced the "Airstream Clipper," which was the first of the classic sausage-shaped, silver aluminum Airstream trailers. It slept four, carried its own water supply, was fitted with electric lights, and cost $1,200.

Today's RVs range from simple trailers and pickup truck "caps" to luxury apartments on wheels. For a "Class A" diesel (the big ones that look like tour buses), you can plunk down $450,000 for a new American Coach "American Revolution" model that measures forty-three feet in length and weighs twenty-two tons. It sleeps six in unrivaled comfort. The kitchen features a two-burner induction cooktop, dishwasher, and refrigerator with icemaker. There's also a washer/dryer so you can stay on the road without worrying about finding a laundromat. In the rear, the master bedroom features a king-size bed, dual nightstands, and a private master bath with a shower with bench seat, a toilet, and vanity with sink and medicine cabinet.

With the rise of RVs, people needed a safe place to park them, and so was born the RV park. Typically, for a fee, an RV park will provide amenities such as an AC power connection, drinking water connection, sewer connection, and even cable TV, phone, and Wi-Fi. Community amenities may include everything you'd find at a conventional resort, such as a restaurant, laundry, social areas, tennis court, or swimming pool. Like any other resort, you make your reservation, drive in, plug in, and relax with your neighbors.

Rocky Mountain National Park has five RV campgrounds. Four of them are seasonal, while the Moraine Park Campground is open year round. Some require reservations, while others are first-come, first-served. If you drive a rolling hotel like the American Revolution, you need to check the maximum length allowed—at forty-three feet it's too long for the Rocky Mountain National Park campgrounds, although you may be able to sneak into Moraine Park, which posts a maximum vehicle length of forty feet.

Motorcycle Clubs
If all you know about motorcycle clubs is what you remember from *The Wild One*, the 1953 biker film starring Marlon Brando and Lee Marvin, you might want to update your thinking. Today, retirees make up a huge chunk of motorcycle riders, and the "gangs" they ride with are a lot friendlier than Marlon Brando's.

Many motorcycle riding clubs are sponsored by various manufacturers, such as the Harley Owners Group and the Honda Riders Club of America. Large national independent motorcycle clubs, such as BMW Riders Association, the Gold Wing Road Riders Association (GWRR), BMW Motorcycle Owners of America, and the STAR Touring and Riding Association provide opportunities for riding and socializing. Other riding clubs exist for a specific purpose, such as the Patriot Guard Riders, who provide escorts for the funerals of military veterans.

An American nonprofit organization of more than 200,000 motorcyclists, the American Motorcyclist Association organizes motorcycling activities and campaigns for the legal rights of motorcyclists. Its mission statement is "to promote the motorcycling lifestyle and protect the future of motorcycling."

For women, Motor Maids is the preeminent women's motorcycle club in North America with over 1,200 members from the United States and Canada. Founded in 1940, the objective of the group is to meet new people, promote safe riding habits, and travel throughout the United States. Every July they have a Motor Maid convention.

Like RV enthusiasts, motorcycle riders have their favorite scenic rides. One of the most popular is along the Pacific Coast Highway from Carmel to Morro Bay, California. The Big Sur section of California's legendary coastal highway stretches 120 miles and has frequent turnouts for enjoying the amazing views. It offers unrivalled attractions including towering redwood forests, crashing surf, beaches populated by lazing seals, and plenty of curves to keep you on your toes. It's part of the extensive Pacific Coast Highway, which extends the length of the California coast from Los Angeles to the Oregon border and beyond.

Another choice ride is River Road, in Texas. It's a seventeen-mile off-road loop through the Valley of the Gods—a highlight of Highway 170 between Candelaria and Presidio, Texas. The River Road follows the Rio Grande on a twisting 115-mile trail past looming cliffs in rainbow shades of reds, purples, and ochers. Other attractions include ancient lava flows and the Fort Leaton State Historic Site, an adobe fortress dating from 1848. This may not be a ride you'll want to take in July or August: it can get mighty hot!

In the summer, try the Peak to Peak National Scenic Byway in Colorado. Only sixty miles long, it combines hairpin turns with some of the most spectacular scenery in the Rockies. As the road crests the Continental Divide in the heart of Rocky Mountain National Park, you'll pass glacial valleys and switchbacks before dropping down to Estes Park. As an added attraction, some old mines along the route allow the public to pan for gold in the creek—for a fee, of course.

Regardless of whether you join a club or go with friends, taking a motorcycle or RV excursion can be a great way to have fun while maintaining your community connections. And who knows—you may like life "on the road" so much that you'll never want to go home!

4. Good Health

Many people believe that the older you get, the sicker *you become*, when in reality, research shows that the older you get, the healthier *you've been*.

During our working years, taking care of ourselves is often the last thing on our list. Many of us are challenged by finding the time to take care of ourselves emotionally and physically, and self-care often boils down to eating and sleeping!

Some people think it's too late, but research shows that it's never too late to improve your health. The body's capacity to get stronger and be healthier and happier is still there even in older years. Aging doesn't necessarily mean a life that is sick, senile, sexless, or inactive. In fact, the opposite is true.

Exercise can help reduce the risk of developing disabilities and diseases as you grow older. Regular movement and exercise is a treatment for many chronic conditions. We've discussed some activities, such as hiking and snowshoeing, that are both rewarding and can help keep you healthy. Following are some others.

Gardening

Gardening is a popular pastime—according to the National Gardening Association (NGA), about three-quarters of households age fifty-five or older participate in some form of lawn and garden activity. At any age, gardening is one of the best activities you can do outdoors. It awakens your connection with nature, stimulates all of the senses, and offers the reward of fresh flowers and delicious herbs and vegetables.

There are things you can do to make gardening easier as you get older. Your back and knees can easily get stiff and sore from kneeling or bending. Waist-high raised beds are one way to eliminate bending and let you get more done in your garden.

Gardening can strengthen your ties to your community if you donate a portion of what you grow. You can plant an extra row in your garden, and then donate the produce to a need-based organization. Crops like squash, corn, tomatoes, and peppers are popular with most people and can be used right away. But the best herbs and vegetables to donate are the ones you have the most luck growing in your garden. Regardless of what you grow, an unexpected surplus can make a big difference in helping feed the hungry.

Sports and Activity Classes
Learning is a joy, and lifelong learning opportunities are an important part of any retirement plan. You can pursue them on your own, or sign up for programs and activities sponsored by your town, retirement community, or church. Painting classes are popular—perhaps you'll become the next George W. Bush!—as are foreign language classes to prepare you for that planned trip abroad. For the literary minded, book clubs are offered at many senior communities and libraries, and community college writing workshops can help you tell your story or write the novel you've always dreamed of. Computer classes are also common, especially those that teach the ins and outs of social media. (According to the Pew Research Center, between 2009 and 2011, use of social media among retirees grew 150%, making it the largest growth in a demographic group.) Seniors have discovered that Facebook and Skype are great ways to bring relatives from distant cities into their living rooms.

Attending lectures by visiting professionals and academics can help you to keep expanding your horizons. You can learn about nature, politics, conservation, art, local history—just about anything, and many programs are either free or discounted for seniors.

Many communities have a wide range of healthy activities, including golf, Tai Chi, yoga, dance classes, and exercise classes. Community centers are not only a great place to stay active but for meeting new people as well. Check local community centers or your local YMCA to see the availability of senior activities.

Swimming is an especially beneficial activity for retirees. It's easy on joints while using all large muscle groups of the body. Swimming even increases bone density, which can reduce the risk of osteoporosis. You can join a swim program at the YMCA or your local health club, or you can swim at a resort or your summer home at the lake. As you plan your retirement, make sure to include your priorities for an active life and make sure you have the resources to accomplish what you want to do.

5. *Spirituality*

The first item in this section was your purpose. By that I meant your obvious, day-to-day purpose—how you wanted to spend your time and energy after getting out of bed each day. During our working lives, work and role-related obligations are what get us going in the morning. As the song goes, "Hi ho, hi ho, it's off to work we go!"

But beyond keeping busy, most people need a deeper reason for being. Like many people, you may ask, what is the purpose of my being here on earth? Why am I here? And where am I going?

Let's face it: there's nothing like an office retirement party or blowing out ninety candles on your birthday cake that better reminds you that you're not going to be around forever. Eventually we're all going to be shuffling off this mortal coil along with the roughly one hundred billion other people who have predeceased us.

Many retirees take comfort in reaffirming their spirituality. This doesn't necessarily mean just going to church more often. In fact, for many retirees, aging provides an opportunity to explore beliefs about the universe and your place in it. Retirement often affords opportunities for seniors to get involved in service to others, to grow spiritually and intellectually, and to provide care to family members.

If you want to explore your spirituality in a structured environment, you might want to plan on visiting a retreat like the Shambhala Mountain Center in Red Feather Lakes, Colorado. At this six-hundred-acre Rocky Mountain retreat you can find your own meditative approach by creating a personal retreat package. The many programs offered range from simple stress-relieving meditation to nature-based programs delving into astronomy or botany. You can stay for any length of time from a weekend to a month and explore contemplative arts, body awareness, personal transformation, or mindful living. Eight miles of trails provide an immersive experience for running, hiking, or snowshoeing, which can lead to the practice of moving or active meditation. Accommodations vary to suit just about any taste or budget, from rustic tent platforms to lodge suites with modern amenities. As for the cuisine, there's something for everyone, from vegetarian and vegan to meat lovers, all the way from Indian to Italian. The best part? There's no cell phone service—you have to truly disconnect!

In this chapter we've presented a brief glimpse of the possibilities that await you in your well-planned retirement. There are many more! To make your retirement dreams come true, it's important to plan ahead. Our good friends Jim and Christine once told us working people should retire *to* something, not just *from* something. This is so true! Working with your qualified retirement planner, you can blend your financial future with your active future, and lay the groundwork for a purposeful retirement filled with personal growth, gratitude, generosity, and a renewed connection to what's really important to you.

Chapter Nine:

Health Care—Planning through the Chaos

According to the U.S. Census Bureau, by 2040 the average life expectancy may be as high as eighty-five. That's the good news. We're living both longer and better. Many of us are staying active, traveling, and even working, in some cases, well into our seventies and eighties.

The bad news is that as we age we become more susceptible to illness, and time takes its toll on our bodies.

Health care costs are rising faster than inflation. According to a 2013 Kaiser Study, health care costs are rising 4% to 6% per year. Another study done by Fidelity Investments believes that a sixty-five-year-old couple can plan on spending $240,000 in out-of-pocket costs during retirement. It's not unusual to see our clients who retire prior to sixty-five spend $1,200 to $1,500 per month for insurance premiums, plus $4,000 to $6,000 in deductibles annually. We recommend clients budget at least $1,000 per month for health care expenses.

In a report by The Center for Economic and Policy Research, a nonpartisan think tank established to promote democratic debate on important economic and social issues that affect people's lives, health care cost growth over the next ten years would be four times as large as the tax increase that Social Security trustees say is needed to keep Social Security solvent for the next seventyfive years. The think tank projects that health care costs will continue to rise faster than GDP.

Consequently, developing a retirement strategy that addresses health care issues may be more problematic than ever and more necessary.

Employer and Group Plans

The purpose of health insurance is to reduce the financial burden that individuals face when illness occurs. By far, most private health insurance is group insurance. Group insurance is usually related to past or current employment of a family member, and is provided by private insurance companies, service plans like Blue Cross/Blue Shield, health maintenance organizations (HMOs), or preferred provider organizations (PPOs). These plans may also offer dental and vision care. Furthermore, as a result of the Consolidated Omnibus Budget Reconciliation Act of 1986 (COBRA), group coverage may be continued for a certain amount of time after the employee leaves the company, provided he or she pays the entire cost of the coverage.

However, employees and retirees should know that private sector employers are not required to promise retiree health benefits. Furthermore, when employers do offer retiree health benefits, nothing in federal law prevents them from cutting or eliminating those benefits unless they have made a specific promise to maintain the benefits.

To understand the terms of employer-provided retiree health benefits, you should first review your plan documents. The summary plan description (SPD) is a summary of the terms of the plan. Employers are required to provide a copy to you within ninety days after you become a participant in the plan. For retirees, the SPD that was in effect when you retired may be the controlling document. You should save a copy of it.

Private Health Insurance
The other 10% of private health insurance is individual health insurance. These plans provide a variety of coverages and renewal provisions, but are generally much more expensive than group plans and must be paid for entirely by the individual.

If you have a high-deductible health plan, I encourage you to contribute to a Health Savings Plan (HSA). An HSA is an account that you can contribute to with either pretax or tax-deductible dollars. An HSA does not require you to use it or lose it within a calendar year. The neat thing about HSAs is that you can pay for qualified health care expenses or allow the money to grow into the future. Any withdrawals from this account to pay for qualified medical expenses are tax free.

I like the idea of paying for medical expenses out of pocket and allowing your HSA contributions to grow tax free for health care–related expenses in retirement. If you are planning on delaying withdrawals for down the road, many HSA plans have investment options. Contribution limits change from year to year, so I recommend that you either check with your HSA provider or the irs.gov website for both limits and rules.

As baby boomers begin to retire en masse, more and more people will look to the government for their basic health care needs. Most people use Medicare; however, Medicare is subject to deductibles, copayments, and other limitations.

In order to adequately prepare for retirement, knowing as much about the various government programs as possible is imperative. Following is an examination of Medicare and Medicaid—two of the most commonly used and yet least understood government health care programs.

Medicare

Medicare is the health insurance arm of Social Security. When you reach sixty-five, you will be eligible for the nation's largest group insurance plan for older Americans, with over thirty-three million members nationwide. Established in 1965 as part of LBJ's Great Society, most Americans are aware of this federal health insurance program. However, most Americans over the age of sixty-five (about 75%, according to a survey by the AARP) admit they know "not much" or "only some" about what Medicare covers and how much it pays in reimbursement. Unfortunately, knowing a little about Medicare can be worse than knowing nothing, since knowing a little may lead a person to false assumptions about the program.

For instance, beneficiaries are required to pay premiums, deductibles, and coinsurance. Indeed, total out-of-pocket health costs for older people average about 15% of their income—the same proportion as before Medicare was enacted, according to the Senate Special Committee on Aging.

Another example of how knowing a little may be worse than knowing nothing is that if you plan to keep working after sixtyfive, you have to apply for Medicare. Enrollment is automatic only for retirees.

Still yet, if you or your spouse needs nursing home care, Medicare will not foot the entire bill. Many people believe that it may provide partial reimbursement in some instances. Medicare, however, defines most situations wherein nursing home care is involved as "custodial." Medicare does not pay for custodial care.

Medicare rules and regulations are not set in stone and, in fact, may change on a political whim, as they did in 1988 when Congress enacted the first major expansion of the program, and then turned right around and repealed the catastrophic care benefits in 1989.

Enrollment in Medicare

When you turn sixty-five you are eligible for Medicare. Almost anyone sixty-five or older can enroll, but if neither you nor your spouse has accumulated enough Social Security or government work credits to be insured, you'll have to buy into the system. If you're already receiving Social Security or railroad retirement benefits, you will automatically be enrolled on your sixty-fifth birthday. If you plan to keep working past sixty-five, however, or if you have to buy into the system, you have to apply.

The Four Parts of Medicare

Medicare consists of four parts:

Part A (hospital insurance), which covers inpatient care, skilled home-health care, hospice care, and some convalescence in a skilled nursing facility.

Part B, which provides medical insurance and helps pay for doctor's services, outpatient procedures, diagnostic tests, durable medical equipment such as wheelchairs, and many other services and supplies not covered under Part A.

Part C (commonly called Medicare Advantage), which are health plan options that are part of the Medicare program, such as HMOs, PPOs, Fee-for-Service Plans, and Medicare Special Needs Plans, and usually include extra benefits and lower co-payments than in the original Medicare plan, but often limit which doctors you may see.

Part D, which covers both brand name and generic prescription drugs. Enrollment is voluntary and requires payment of a monthly premium, but you won't find comparable benefits at a lower rate.

Participating Providers

Medicare pays 80% of fees that it defines as reasonable; you are responsible for the remaining 20% (called coinsurance). If your doctor, nursing home, or home health agency charges more than the amount approved by Medicare, you will have to pay those charges as well as the coinsurance. Physicians are prohibited from charging more than 15% above the amount approved by Medicare. One way to avoid out-of-pocket expenses is to use doctors and suppliers who have agreed to accept Medicare's approved amount as payment in full. Such doctors or suppliers can charge you only for the portion of the Part B deductible you have not met and for the coinsurance. More than 40% of the nation's doctors accept what is called Medicare assignment. Those who do can save you time as well as money because they submit the claim forms. For the names and addresses of participating doctors and suppliers, consult the Medicare Participating Physician/Supplier Directory, available free from your Medicare carrier.

What Medicare Doesn't Cover

Medicare does *not* cover certain kinds of care, charges, or supplies. (Most private insurance policies don't cover these items, either.)

Here are some examples:

- Private-duty nursing
- Care in a skilled-nursing home after one hundred days each year. (Skilled nursing facilities have staff and equipment to provide round-the-clock nursing care or rehabilitation services prescribed by a doctor.)
- Custodial services (help in walking, getting in and out of bed, eating, and dressing), whether in nursing facility or at home
- Intermediate nursing home care. (Such care may require the skills of a nurse but at a less intensive level than that given in a skilled-nursing facility.)
- Physician fees above Medicare's approved amounts

- Care received outside the U.S., except under limited circumstances in Canada and Mexico
- Dental care or dentures, check-ups, most routine immunizations, cosmetic surgery, routine foot care, and examinations for and the cost of eyeglasses or hearing aids

Medicare can be difficult to understand and navigate. I encourage you to meet with a Medicare advisor. We provide our planning clients access to a Medicare advisor who was a former State Health Insurance and Assistance Programs (SHIPs) counselor. However, another option is to contact your state's SHIPs agency to talk to a counselor.

The SHIPs programs provide seniors with one-on-one counseling to help them take full advantage of their benefits. All states have a toll-free telephone number, which can be found at payingforseniorcare.com.

Medicare Supplemental Insurance

These policies are intended to provide additional health care benefits to your basic Medicare coverage. They should never be purchased in place of broader forms of coverage. Many supplemental policies provide important health care benefits; some offer more than they eventually plan to deliver.

Often called Medigap policies, these plans are designed to help fill some of the gaps in Medicare coverage. In accordance with regulations established by the National Association of Insurance Commissioners (NAIC), every Medigap policy is required to provide coverage for the following items:

- Either *all* of the Medicare hospital deductible or *none* of it; this either/or requirement makes it easier for consumers to compare Medicare supplemental insurance policies.
- The Medicare hospital coinsurance, plus 90% of per diem hospital expenses not covered by Medicare, up to a maximum of one year
- The blood transfusion deductible, unless the blood is replaced by the policyholder
- The 20% co-payment for physician services, after the policyholder pays the Part B deductible

More than the specific details, it's important to know that minimum standards apply to every Medicare supplemental insurance policy sold in the United States. In general, you'll never need more than one Medigap policy; buying two only wastes money on duplicate minimum coverage. Seniors have been the victims of what consumer advocate David Horowitz calls "medicrap abuse." While the NAIC has drafted model regulations to crack down on such abuses, buyers should still beware. To help you protect yourself against fast-talking sales people, you need to read between the lines of these commonly used, often misleading sales pitches:

- THE PITCH: A person claiming to be a Social Security Medicare worker tries to sell you a Medigap policy. Don't believe it. Representatives of these federal programs don't sell or service such insurance.
- THE PITCH: A salesperson explains that Medicare does not cover extended stays in a nursing home, then pitches a

Medigap policy. REALITY: Her statement is true as far as it goes: Medicare helps pay for care in a skilled nursing facility for only one hundred days and does not cover stays of any length in intermediate or custodial care nursing homes. But the agent has misled you by implying that Medigap policies cover lengthy nursing home stays. They don't! Medigap policies do *not* pay for custodial or intermediate care at home or in a nursing home, which are the types of care older persons are most likely to need for long-term illnesses. Consumers can purchase insurance policies that cover long-term care, but these are presently distinct from Medigap policies and do not supplement Medicare hospital and physician benefits.

- THE PITCH: A Medigap insurance agent asks whether you'd be interested in a policy that "prevents you from becoming a burden to your spouse or children." With your worst fears aroused, you have difficulty resisting the sales pitch. REALITY: The implication is that Medigap insurance offers coverage for long-term care. Once again, it *doesn't*. If you're worried about what will happen if you ever need extended care, discuss your concerns with family members and explore options such as purchasing long-term care insurance or buying into a continuing-care retirement community.

- THE PITCH: An insurance rep asks whether you'd like coverage for prescription drugs. You would, because your current Medigap policy doesn't provide this benefit. Some higher priced Medigap policies provide more insurance than the law requires—for prescription drugs, physician fees in excess of Medicare-approved charges, or other benefits. Monthly premiums for these policies pay for the standard Medigap insurance plus the additional coverage.

REALITY: If you want broader coverage to supplement Medicare, upgrade your current Medigap policy, or exchange it for one that fits your needs. If you change policies, check for clauses on preexisting conditions that may limit your coverage. Don't buy an extra policy; you'll waste money duplicating insurance.

Before you buy any Medigap policy, ask yourself whether you really need it. If you have group medical coverage through a current or former employer, you probably don't need supplemental insurance. Ditto for people who receive both Medicare and Medicaid (Medicare providers are required to accept the Medicaid reimbursement as payment in full), and for HMO enrollees who incur only limited out-of-pocket expenses.

Every Medigap policy must follow federal and state laws designed to protect you, and each must be clearly identified as "Medicare Supplemental Insurance." Insurance companies can sell you only a "standardized" policy. All policies offer the same basic benefits, but some offer additional benefits so you can choose which one meets your needs. There are a full range of benefit options described as Medigap plans that range from plans "A" through "N."

There is another class of plans called Medicare Advantage Plans. These plans are typically offered by a private health care provider and accept what Medicare pays them and don't charge the insured additional premiums.

Every year there is an open enrollment period to make changes to your plan. The open enrollment period is October 15th through December 7th. Determine if you need to make any changes prior to open enrollment. I believe the best way to determine this is to sit down with a qualified Medicare advisor.

Protecting Yourself Against Long-Term-Care Costs

Conservative estimates are that one in every three persons over sixty-five will enter a nursing home at some point in their lives.

According to the U.S. Department of Health and Human Services, the average cost for long-term care is $265 per day for a semiprivate room in a nursing home. It's $295 per day for a private room and $140 per day for assisted living.

After only thirteen weeks in a nursing home, 70% of older persons living alone become poor; within a year, over 90% are impoverished, according to the U.S. House Select Committee on Aging. The outlook for married couples is only somewhat less bleak: one out of two couples become impoverished after one spouse has spent just half a year in a nursing home.

Discouraging as they are, these statistics say nothing of the personal sacrifices and human suffering that lie behind them. What can you do to protect yourself against the high cost of long-term care? The answers are incomplete and will continue to be so until we as a nation establish a comprehensive long-term health-care program. In the meantime, in addition to advocating that your legislators support such a program, you need to plan ahead to safeguard yourself against catastrophic health care costs.

Develop a Medicaid Plan

If you need nursing home care, chances are that either you or Medicaid will foot the bill. Don't count on Medicare because its nursing home benefit is extremely limited. And don't pin your hopes on private long-term-care insurance. While such policies have improved over time, good ones are still hard to come by and may be prohibitively expensive. Veterans Administration benefits? Don't expect much: The nursing home coverage is limited and generally won't last longer than six months. That leaves you and Medicaid, and by the time Medicaid starts paying, you've already paid—and paid dearly.

Obviously, unless you've planned ahead, you or your spouse can wind up virtually broke. So-called divestment planning is often used when one person wants to qualify for Medicaid nursing home benefits as quickly as possible while preserving life savings. Typically, middle-income persons benefit most from divestment or Medicaid planning; people with very low incomes will quickly qualify for Medicaid if they need nursing home care, while the more affluent can afford to pay the nursing home tab.

One caveat to divestment planning is that it may help qualify you or a loved one only for nursing home care that is substandard. It shouldn't come as a big surprise that the quality of nursing home care provided to Medicaid residents is lower than that provided to private-pay patients. Consequently, most people prefer not to have to go on Medicaid. It is also a question of ethics: should taxpayers pay for a person's care if they have assets to pay for all or some of the costs?

I'll briefly discuss some of the most common divestment strategies to familiarize you with your options. You should, however, seek professional financial planning and legal advice before you jump in, as many variables can come into play in specific cases.

Hold Assets in Exempt Form

Medicaid applicants can keep certain assets, including their home and car, and still qualify for benefits. They can also legally use nonexempt assets, such as money in a savings account or CD, to pay for exempt assets. This way, instead of paying the nursing home all of their savings, they've invested in their home, car, and household goods. So pay off your mortgage and fix up your car!

Transfer Assets Sixty Months or More before a Nursing Home Stay

One way to increase the likelihood of qualifying for Medicaid nursing home benefits is to give a portion of your assets to your siblings, other relatives, or friends. If you do this at least sixty months—that's five years—before entering a nursing home, the transferred assets will not be counted in determining Medicaid eligibility. Be careful; if a person disposes of assets for less than fair market value within thirty months of a nursing home stay, states can delay eligibility for Medicaid.

Shuffle Assets between Spouses

Because a couple's combined life savings are counted in determining eligibility for Medicaid, this strategy will not help the nursing home spouse qualify more quickly for benefits. However, it may help preserve the couple's assets if the spouse living at home dies first.

Seek a Court Order

One way for a spouse at home to retain more assets and income than state law normally allows is to seek a court order authorizing the additional support.

"The court order can go so far as to award the healthy spouse all of the community and even some or all of the separate property," wrote Marc Hankin, in Fulbright & Jaworski's Elder Law Newsletter. "Whatever property the court order allocates to a healthy spouse need not be spent for the other spouse's nursing home costs, and there is no limit on the amount that the court can award. Similarly the court order can require the unhealthy spouse to pay the healthy spouse's support even if it exceeds the Medicaid limit, and even if it comes from Social Security or pension benefits."

Set Up a Trust Sixty Months or More before Entering a Nursing Home

When you establish a trust, you transfer ownership of certain property and other assets to a trustee, who agrees to manage the resources according to the terms of the trust document. New rules have made it more difficult to establish a trust so that its assets will not be counted in determining Medicaid eligibility. But it's not impossible, provided you get legal and/or financial planning advice.

Buy a Long-Term-Care Insurance Policy

Another method for protecting yourself against the high cost of long-term care is to buy private long-term-care insurance, which should cover nursing home stays, assisted living, and home health care services. People whose income and assets are fairly modest should think twice before buying long-term-care insurance because they would quickly qualify for Medicaid benefits should they need to stay in a nursing home.

There are other issues involved in this strategy, including what is and isn't covered, to what extent, and the conditions under which a specific thing may be covered. Oftentimes policies are set up to look good on paper but have stipulations as to the conditions and circumstances of the coverage.

Often insurance agents try to sell you more coverage than what you may need or afford. An agent should consider your personal resources such as direct income (Social Security, rents, royalties, and pensions) and other income-producing assets (IRAs, 401ks, and securities). We often find that while a private room may cost almost $300 per day, a client could and should be looking at a benefit of a lesser amount because of their other resources.

Another consideration is the benefit period. A longer benefit period means higher premiums. While the average stay in a nursing home is less than three years, keep in mind that some stays may last for a couple of months while some may last for years. I look at this way—if you've got yourself covered either through insurance or personal savings for, let's say, three years, you've covered 95% of your risk. Certainly long-term care could last beyond three years, but the odds of that is pretty remote.

In cases where you may have excess retirement capital, you may want to earmark some of the funds for the potential need for future long-term-care needs rather than buying insurance.

I've experienced long-term-care insurance agents promoting the purchase of single-pay premium policies. Often this is recommended prior to determining if the money that will be needed to pay the premium is going to be needed for future income needs. There is really no way to determine if you need to purchase insurance without including long-term-care planning in your financial or retirement plan.

Attach a Long-Term-Care Rider to a Life Insurance Policy

This arrangement allows all or a portion of the policy's death benefit to be prepaid in monthly installments to a living policyholder should he or she enter a nursing home. Long-term-care riders can cost as little as $100 per year on a $100,000 universal policy. ("Stand-alone" long-term-care insurance policies may cost ten times that amount.) There are several caveats involved, such as tax issues and the common practice of bundling different types of insurance into one package, which frequently results in purchasing coverage that you may not need. As with virtually every option, consult an experienced professional before buying.

Join a Continuing Care Retirement Community

Most people want to age in place, but for those who don't, one option is a continuing care retirement community (CCRC). Many CCRCs offer guaranteed health care for the resident's lifetime. They do this by offering independent living, assisted living, and nursing home care all within one community. As your health changes you can move from one type of residence to another.

There is a significant cost to this sort of convenience. Entrance fees can run anywhere from $100,000 to $1 million, and monthly fees can range from $3,000 to $5,000 or more for couples.

Currently an estimated 600,000 people live in CRCCs. Experts say many residents and prospective residents overlook the financial risks they take when entering a CCRC. Since you won't own anything, you could lose your entire investment if the facility goes broke or if you decide to move down the road for whatever reason. Or you could find that by the time you need skilled nursing care, the facility has deteriorated considerably.

You may enter a CCRC because it's new and the property is attractive and its food is excellent, only to find out later that the skilled nursing facility is not particularly good or the property itself isn't maintained and falls to disrepair. In this case, you made the wrong choice.

While initially a CCRC may seem attractive, don't overlook the risks. If you are thinking about buying into a CCRC, I highly recommend doing your homework. The Financial Advisory Council of the Commission on Rehabilitation Facilities (CARF) and Continuing Care Accreditation Commission (CCAC) produces two publications about the financial performance of CCRCs. These publications can be purchased on the CARF online bookstore.

Chapter Ten:

Estate Planning —Passing It On

One of the most difficult parts of retirement planning can be preparing for the distribution of assets after your death. No one likes to think about the inevitable, much less plan for it. The truth is, however, without such plans your retirement plan would be incomplete and could unduly burden loved ones when the inevitable happens. Understandably, procrastination is the biggest problem most people have with this particular area of financial planning.

Estate planning is the process of setting forth binding instructions so that when you die, your personal property and other assets are distributed according to your wishes, and with a minimum of bother and expense for your heirs. I suggest, however, that estate planning is not about death; it's about life. It allows you to pass on a part of your life for the care of others. Think of it as a final act of love.

159

Most people think the process by which assets and property passes from one person to another at death is a straightforward, relatively direct, and simple procedure. Unfortunately, without a well-conceived and properly administered plan, the process will be neither smooth nor swift. It can quickly turn into a nightmare for survivors if one's affairs are in disorder or plans are unclear. Moreover, each state has its own set of rules governing the disposition of assets upon death, so a proper plan must recognize and conform to these laws.

There are enough estate planning approaches to fill up a separate book. To keep things concise, in this chapter I'll examine some of the most important basic planning tools, including wills, various trusts, joint tenancies, letters of last instruction, and advanced directives. Armed with this information, you should have a good basic understanding of your estate planning options.

Getting Started: Name Your Beneficiaries

To properly plan for the distribution of your property and assets, you first need to decide who should inherit your assets. If you're married, you need to decide how much and what your spouse will get. There are laws designed to protect surviving spouses, and if you die without a will or living trust, state law will dictate how much your spouse will get. Even if you have a will or living trust, and you leave your spouse less than state law specifies, the law will see to it that the surviving spouse receives his or her share as provided for by state law.

After you've decided how much your spouse should receive, you need to decide whether your children will share equally in your estate.

Also, do you want to name your grandchildren (or any others) as beneficiaries? And finally, do you want to leave any assets to charity? Once you've considered these issues, it's time to decide who gets what. While this may seem fairly straightforward, considering the various possibilities can be quite complicated. For instance, if you own a business and some of your children are active in the business, should the stock in the business pass to them? And if so, should you compensate any other children with assets of comparable value? Or if you own rental property, should it pass to all beneficiaries—or just the ones who are able to manage the properties? In each instance, you need to keep in mind that a divorce can throw the whole situation into chaos unless you plan for such exigencies.

Other issues to consider are *when* and *how* beneficiaries should inherit assets. Things to keep in mind include the age and maturity of the beneficiaries, the size of your estate and your (and your spouse's) need for income during your life times and, of course, tax implications. Outright bequests are simple, flexible, and offer some tax advantages, but you have no control over what happens to them next. Trusts are useful when beneficiaries are young and/or immature, if your estate is large, or for tax planning purposes, and can provide asset management capabilities.

Calculate Your Net Worth

Once you have considered these issues, the next step is to calculate your net worth. Add up your cash, stocks and bonds, notes and mortgages, annuities, retirement benefits, personal residence, other real estate, partnership interests, automobiles, artwork, jewelry, and collectibles. Also, if you own an insurance policy when you die, the proceeds on that policy will usually be included in your estate. And make sure to include your spouse's assets as well. The legal documents you select for distributing your estate will depend on your net worth, so it's important to be as accurate as possible.

After you've calculated your current net worth, project the future value of what your estate may be worth when you are likely to die.

Next, subtract any debts, any assets that will pass to charity, and any assets that will pass to your spouse. The net number you come up with is your *taxable estate*.

The next step is to find out what the current estate tax rules are so you can take steps to minimize these taxes if necessary. In some cases—specifically, if your net worth exceeds $5.49 million through 2017—your best strategy for reducing estate tax is to seek advice from an estate attorney or a qualified estate advisor. I like to stress the importance of planning to preserve one's unified tax credit and not need it than to need it and not have it because one cannot resurrect the credit from the grave.

You can also check my website at www.TownsendRetirement.com for the latest tax and financial information; it's much easier to navigate than the IRS site.

Now let's take a look at some of the tools that are available for distributing your assets.

Write Your Will

The will is the most important tool in an estate plan. For many people, a will constitutes the foundation of their distribution strategy. Your will designates how and to whom your assets will be distributed when you die. It also allows you to name an executor to carry out the terms of your will and to appoint a guardian for any dependent children. It allows your heirs to settle your estate more easily, and can save money in taxes and other settlement expenses. It can also continue specific programs you initiated during your life, such as gifts to charity. If properly prepared, your will can help protect your estate and beneficiaries from shrinkage caused by inefficient transfers, income and estate taxes, and other costs.

If not properly prepared, however, a will can be more costly than having none at all. A contested will that results in litigation may consume most or all of the estate in question. The advantages of a will are that it provides standardized procedures and court supervision, and the claims period for creditors can be shorter than for a living trust.

If you choose to use a will to distribute your assets—rather than, for example, placing your entire estate in a trust, because most trusts aren't probated, as discussed below—it will be necessary for your estate to go through probate. Probate is a court-supervised process to protect the rights of creditors and beneficiaries and to ensure the orderly and timely transfer of assets. There are six steps in the probate process:

1. Notification of interested parties. Most states require disclosure of the estate's approximate value as well as the names and

addresses of interested parties. These include all beneficiaries named in the will, natural heirs, and creditors.

2. Appointment of an executor. If you haven't named an executor, the court will appoint one to oversee the estate's liquidation and distribution. This is why it behooves you to name the executor you want.

3. Accumulation of assets. Essentially, all assets you owned or controlled at the time of your death need to be accounted for.

4. Payment of claims. The type and length of notice required to establish a deadline for creditors to file their claims varies by state. If a creditor does not file its claim on time, the claim generally is barred.

5. Filing of tax returns. This includes final income and estate taxes.

6. Distribution of residuary estate. After the estate has paid debts and taxes, the executor can distribute the remaining assets to the beneficiaries and close the estate.

A will can be a good idea because it standardizes procedures and provides court supervision. Also, the creditor claims limitation period is often shorter than for a living trust. However, probate is time-consuming, potentially expensive, and public. An alternative to this process is a living trust.

Living Trusts

Trusts are excluded from the probate process because the assets in the trust technically don't belong to you—they already belong to the beneficiary of the trust. Thus after you die, there doesn't need to be a court transfer of ownership of those assets.

A living trust is a way to transfer property while an individual is still alive. Property placed in trust avoids the complex probate proceeding, allows quick distribution to your heirs, eliminates probate fees and costs, and saves substantial death taxes. To create a living trust, you transfer title to real estate, stocks, bonds, bank accounts, and other assets to a trust while you're still alive. You also designate a trustee who is responsible for managing your assets. (You may also designate yourself as trustee while you are alive, and retain the right to revoke the trust and appoint and remove trustees.)

Trust documents also allow you to name a successor trustee, who steps in to manage and distribute your assets after you die or should you become incapacitated. If you set up a revocable living trust, you can change it at any time. An irrevocable living trust cannot be altered unless the court determines that its provisions are unworkable or that they frustrate the trust's general purpose. Unlike wills, living trusts do not go through probate; thus, your estate may be settled faster and with less expense.

Also, the trust does not need to file an income tax return until after you die. Instead, you pay the tax on any income the trust earns as if you never created the trust. Moreover, your assets are not exposed to public record.

However, there are disadvantages to a living trust.

Transferring titles to homes, bank accounts, and business and other investments into the name of the trust can be cumbersome and time consuming. When refinancing a home, some lenders require that the house title be taken out of a trust, although it can be placed back in afterward. Also, the legal fees for setting up a living trust tend to be substantially higher than they are for preparing a will. You will also still need to have a short will, often called a "pour-over" will.

For these reasons, living trusts may not be the best option for people with few assets.

Stretch IRA

If you are like millions of Americans, you probably already know that an IRA is a powerful retirement tool. What you may not know is that an IRA can be a giant tax bomb at the death of the account owner. However, a Stretch IRA can leave a legacy to your heirs while reducing and deferring the impact of taxes.

There is a good chance that your IRA represents your largest asset. There is also a good chance that the entire balance will be subject to state and federal income taxes upon your death. Depending on your balance, it can be taxed at the top income rates, leaving your heirs perhaps half of the original balance.

Taxes may not be the only problem. The balance could easily become part of the marital property of your heirs and subject to lawsuits, which includes divorces. How are your heirs with money? Will the money be prudently managed and spent? Would you like to have some say on how your IRA is handled? The solution to these questions is establishing a Stretch IRA provision within your estate documents.

A Stretch IRA allows your IRA to continue growing tax-deferred less required minimum distributions (RMD). The beneficiaries to your IRA will be required to take an RMD annually based on their age; however, any balances will continue to grow tax deferred.

Other benefits include:

✓ The IRA balance never enters marital property.

✓ Helps your heirs to manage their inheritance.

✓ Can provide lifetime income to your heirs.

✓ The IRA balance is protected from lawsuits.

The Stretch IRA is established through a trust that has special language that will incorporate IRA distribution requirements along with how you want your beneficiaries to receive distributions. If you are married you can name your spouse as a primary beneficiary and any other heirs as secondary beneficiaries.

The language in the trust will provide the income to anyone you want, including your children, grandchildren, or any other family members, friends, or charitable organizations. The IRA can be professionally managed by your investment advisor and administered by a corporate trustee.

Legacy Planning

Over the years I have seen many clients' children blow through their inheritances in a matter of months. This is especially troublesome to me when these same clients lived their retirement years in a way so that they could leave their children an inheritance.

Have you given much thought to your legacy, or if you'll even have one? Would you like to see some of your goals, dreams, aspirations, and financial assets played forward? Do you want to be remembered? If so, you'll need a plan.

Many families have a history that should be shared with future generations. This is where a multigenerational trust and family love letter has a role.

Legacy planning is not just for the rich and famous. We all have a legacy, whether planned or not. When thinking of family and future generations, you may want to leave a meaningful legacy.

Legacy planning is an extension of estate planning, and allows you to provide a multigenerational benefit to your heirs and charitable organizations. Legacy planning can help you build a legacy by using wealth in positive ways and passing on your values to future generations.

Legacy planning requires some real thought. As an example, one of our clients did not want to enable their two daughters and their families because of poor estate planning. Their legacy trust distributed 2% of its corpus annually with a cap rate. Another 1% was distributed to their family foundation. The idea behind this was twofold. First, they didn't want their daughters or future generations to be dependent on the trust. They thought it was important that their heirs worked and contributed to society.

Second, they wanted their family to be involved in philanthropy. With proper investment management, the trust could continue for many generations.

What's important to them may not be important to you, and that's OK. You should have your own goals and objectives, which can be part of your own legacy planning.

The trust structure should protect your financial legacy from creditors, predators, in-laws, and outlaws!

Testamentary Trusts

A testamentary trust is created by your will and becomes effective after you die. They offer many of the same tax avoidance advantages of living trusts. In addition, they can:

✓ Be used to eliminate the necessity for guardianships in the case of minor beneficiaries

✓ Create a life income for older beneficiaries such as a spouse, with a gift of the principal to another at the beneficiary's death, thus avoiding successive transfer taxes

✓ Provide for discretion and flexibility with regard to the trustee's power to distribute trust income and principal, which would not be possible with a direct will bequest

✓ Appropriately restrict the use of the trust property by the beneficiary, and incorporate spendthrift provisions that protect the property from dissipation by the beneficiary and from absorption by his or her creditors

✓ Ensure that the decedent controls the disposition of the remainder interest in the trust at the death of the beneficiary

Testamentary trusts must, however, go through the probate process.

Joint Tenancy

Joint tenancy with a right of survivorship is the most common type of joint ownership. In joint tenancy, two persons own property—such as real estate, bank accounts, or investments—in both names. When one co-tenant dies, the other becomes sole owner of the entire property. The surviving tenant is entitled to the property without probate. Keep in mind that you or your co-tenant may have a parting of the ways, and your property may be sold out from under you.

Another drawback is that if a parent puts a child on the deed as joint tenant, the property becomes subject to attachment for the debts of the child. Also, the first joint tenant to die cannot dispose of the property under his or her will, and the surviving tenant is under no legal obligations to share the property with other heirs. Because of these factors, it's best to seek legal advice before placing large assets under joint tenancy.

Letter of Last Instruction

A letter of last instruction can make transferring your property to your heirs a much smoother and easier proposition. Designed to be opened at death, the letter should include the location of:

- Your will or trust instructions
- Birth and marriage certificates
- Insurance policies
- Bank passbooks and numbers
- Proof of ownership or property, checking accounts, credit cards, cars, houses, stocks, retirement benefits

Thoughtful estate planning is absolutely essential no matter how big your estate. In fact, it may not be that large now, but could easily double or triple during retirement, thus making it difficult to protect if you bequeath your share to your spouse.

Other things to consider is how you want your estate distributed. Do you want your estate to go directly to your kids, which could allow your estate to enter your children's marital property? Should there be a divorce, your ex-son-in-law or daughter-in-law has the chance to walk away with a chunk of your estate.

Or do you want your estate to stay in your bloodline and go to your grandchildren should there be any money left after the death of your children? Or, how about a future spouse?

There are an infinite number of scenarios. What I'd like to stress is that one doesn't have to have a large estate to benefit from good estate planning. In fact, taxes are only one part of it. If you'd like to keep your estate out of probate and control the distribution of your estate to make sure your children and grandchildren are protected from current, future, or former spouses, you might want to consider the many benefits of a living trust.

Advance Directives for Protecting Your Assets

Durable Powers of Attorney

One of the most useful tools for not only protecting your assets but handling affairs that you may not be physically or emotionally able to do late in life is a durable power of attorney. This legal instrument allows you to transfer as much or as little power as you want. For example, you can authorize another person to manage your property or simply to sell your car. You can also stipulate how long you want the power of attorney to remain in effect, and you can cancel at any time.

A durable power of attorney can be used to instruct someone to make health care decisions on your behalf should you become disabled, including the kind and intensity of health care. Some states, however, restrict the use of durable powers of attorney to financial matters, so before you execute the necessary paperwork, check the rules, regulations, and restrictions in your state

Medical Directives (Living Wills)

A living will is a directive to physicians and family members that you *not* be given extraordinary treatment if it will only prolong your inevitable death. In the event you are unable to express your wishes, your attending physician is legally obligated to carry out the terms of your living will. There are severe limitations on living wills, and they vary from state to state. Most lawyers and physicians agree that a durable medical power of attorney is better.

Choosing Your Estate Planning Team

Before you start making plans, give serious thought to several important issues. First off, who should draw up your will or living trust? While you will probably want to consult your financial advisor and planner during the planning stages, you will absolutely want to have an attorney who specializes in estate issues draw up any legal documents that you may need.

Next you'll need to choose someone to administer the disposition of your estate, such as an executor or, if you have a living trust, a trustee. You can have anyone from a friend or family member or an institution serving in these capacities. He or she (or it) will, after your death, administer your estate and distribute the assets to your beneficiaries. They will also make certain tax decisions, pay estate debts or expenses, ensure all life insurance and retirement plan benefits are received, fill out necessary tax returns, and pay the appropriate federal and state income taxes as well any applicable estate tax.

Needless to say, you'll want to choose someone who is responsible, willing, and able. It's probably not a good idea to choose someone who is a partner in your business, as he or she may have a conflict of interest. Also, second spouses or children from a previous marriage may have conflicting interests. You'll also want to choose an alternate so that if for some reason your primary choice can't fulfill their responsibilities, you have someone to handle the situation.

Another option of which many people are unaware is a professional fiduciary. Being named as an executor may be an honor, but it's a huge responsibility. A person you appoint as your executor who doesn't have any prior experience can feel overwhelmed. Not only are multiple filings and accounting required, but the executor will also have to deal with family. If your executor is a family member, this can be especially difficult.

A professional fiduciary can be an individual or company with experience as an executor or trustee. In addition to experience, they should be bonded as well. Typically their fees will be substantially less than an attorney. Perhaps the biggest benefit they offer is dealing with family members!

If you have children who are not of age, you will also want to select a guardian in case your spouse is also incapacitated. In addition to the well-being of your children, you also have some financial considerations to address. Is the proposed guardian capable of managing your children's assets? Is he or she financially capable? (You may want to think about compensating them even if they're financially comfortable.) How will the guardian determine your children's living costs?

You will also want to transfer quite a few assets that we haven't already discussed. For instance, the contents of safe deposit boxes. Usually the bank seals the box as soon as it is notified of the death and opens it only in the presence of the estate's personal representative. Also, if savings bonds are jointly owned, the surviving spouse can immediately cash in E bonds. If H and E bonds are registered in the deceased's name but payable on death to the surviving spouse, they must be sent to the Federal Reserve.

Other assets that you'll want to make sure are properly transferred and/or are applied for include Social Security benefits, employee benefits, and any insurance that your family may not have known about.

Estate Taxes

Estate taxes can be brutal. If your estate is more than the exemption amount, a significant portion of it may go to the government as taxes. Here are the basics for 2017:

- The lifetime exclusion amount against the estate tax is $5.49 million and a 40% top federal estate tax rate.
- The lifetime generation-skipping transfer (GST) tax exemption is $5.49 million and a 40% top federal GST tax rate.
- The *annual* gift tax exclusion is $14,000. This applies to gifts to one person. You can give multiple people gifts up to this amount without paying a gift tax.
- The *lifetime* gift tax exemption is $5.49 million and a 40% top federal gift tax rate.

President Trump has stated that he wants to repeal the estate tax completely, benefitting those with estates over $5.49 million, but as of this writing it hasn't happened yet.

In order to make a rough projection of your potential estate tax exposure, take the value of your estate, net of any debts. Then subtract any assets that will pass to charity on your death; if you are married and your spouse is a U.S. citizen, subtract any assets that will pass to him or her. (Those assets qualify for the marital deduction and avoid estate taxes until the surviving spouse dies.) The net number is your taxable estate.

You have available a great many strategies to minimize your estate tax exposure. A good financial planner can be invaluable in terms of helping you prepare your estate to avoid losing a substantial chunk of it to the government instead of passing it on to your loved ones. Moreover, with the incessant tweaking of public policy by elected officials, a good financial planner can keep you abreast of important changes, and can help you and your loved ones retain your precious assets.

Chapter Eleven:

Have a Written Plan

Will you be ready for retirement? If you don't have a plan, the answer will probably be no. According to a recent study by the Employee Benefit Research Institute, nearly 73% of workers have no idea how much money they'll need to be able to live their preretirement lifestyle.

Most people I talk to have a good idea of how they want to spend their retirement, whether it be soaking in the sun on a Florida beach, traveling to far-off places, golfing, playing tennis, spending time with family, or even donating their time to their favorite causes. Few of them, however, have a specific plan that can make those dreams come true. Fewer still have created a detailed written plan that lists goals and objectives, and projects and tracks performance.

Americans are eternal optimists, especially when it comes to their own retirement. Most of us hope for the best, shoot from the hip, and figure everything will be fine. While the key for a secure retirement is *planning*, too many never do it.

Not planning is the number one reason for failure. People today need to plan more than previous generations because they'll be living longer. I know you've heard me say this in earlier chapters, but it's certainly worth saying again: the longer you live, the longer you are *expected* to live. So many people tell me that had they known they were going to live to be the age they are, they would have saved more money and done a better job planning.

In fact, according to the Retirement Confidence survey, 40% of workers who did a retirement plan made changes in their retirement planning as a result; 64% said they started to save more, 26% changed their investment allocations; while smaller percentages researched new methods of saving for retirement and worked on reducing debt.

We need to create a culture of being better savers and investors. We need to develop an attitude of "if it's meant to be, it's up to me." And it starts with having a plan.

Keep in mind that planning is not about how much money you have; rather, it's about having what you'll need to be happy and fulfilled for the rest of your life.

Your plan should include:

- **A strategy to lower your taxes**. You've probably heard Ben Franklin's maxim, "A penny saved is a penny earned." This can certainly be applied to taxes. Most CPAs are great at preparing tax returns but rarely sit down with their clients and work on tax reduction planning. Think about it, if you can reduce your taxes by a couple of thousand dollars, this is an extra couple of thousand that you can save for retirement or spend on your family or yourself.

- **An investment analysis and strategy.** Since your investments are the engine that will power your retirement, doesn't it make sense to have a better understanding of how investments work? Will your dividends provide you enough income to cover your withdrawals? Make sure that your current investments will get you where you want to go.

- **An analysis of your income sources.** Your starting point should be figuring out your direct income sources such as Social Security, pensions, rents, and the like. For many people, this will be the staple in their predictable income. Knowing whether these sources include cost of living adjustments will also be important.

- **An analysis of how long your money will last.** Based on the conversations that I have had with retirees and preretirees, this is probably the number one concern. Often I find that when people see that they are going to receive a sizable amount of money when they retire, they assume that little planning is needed. However, in many cases I've seen these same people deplete their retirement accounts in a relatively short period of time. The reason? Many are unrealistic with how much they can safely withdraw, while others may not have an appropriate asset allocation. If you are too conservative, most likely your investments will be depleted over time due to inadequate interest or yield to support their withdraw rate or to keep up with inflation. On the other hand, if you are too aggressive, the short-term volatility may force you to sell off shares at a loss, and if this continues for long, you will run out of money.

- **An insurance needs analysis.** Do you have the appropriate amount of life insurance to pay for final expenses, pay off debt, and perhaps, most importantly, provide supplemental income if there is a surviving spouse? Is your retirement savings at risk if there is a serious illness or if one spouse needs assisted living or nursing home care? Often I find that people may carry insurances that they don't need and no insurance where it is needed.

- **Estate planning.** While this item is listed last, it's certainly not least. Having a good estate plan in place will make all the difference in the world for simplifying the distribution of your estate after your death. But what a lot of people don't realize is that it can help manage your affairs in your older years or if you become incompetent or incapacitated.

An often overlooked insurance policy is an umbrella policy. This policy extends the liability insurance coverage that you have on your cars and your home. Your car is the most lethal weapon you own, and in a blink of an eye an accident can wipe you out financially.

Your property and casualty agent should be able to help you with how much you should consider. Minimally I believe you should carry a million dollars of coverage. It's relatively cheap, so don't sell yourself short.

I have spoken with many people in various age groups who are working with financial advisors to discuss their own experiences with retirement planning and how their lives changed once they sat down with a financial advisor. While each had different definitions of retirement, all agreed on one thing: No matter what your ideal retirement entails, you need to have a plan.

Case Study: Robert and Julie Hall, ages 67 and 66

One would assume that a husband with a degree in finance and a wife who was a high school principal would have their retirement plan in place from an early age. But Robert and Julie didn't consult with a financial advisor until about five years before they both retired.

Why the wait? "We were so busy working and raising a family, and we didn't want to think about it," said Robert. "We were far more interested in everything else that was going on in our lives than in our personal finances."

In fact, part of the reason they hadn't placed retirement on their list of priorities was that they had always made a good living and never gave too much thought about retiring. After all, when they were in their forties and even fifties, the thought of retirement seemed so far away.

Sure, Robert and Julie had made a few investments along the way. Back in the 1980s they ventured into owning several rentals. Not all were good investments. "We went through a few years in the mideighties when there was a glut of vacancies because many people in the area were losing their jobs due to the oil bust and were moving out of Colorado," said Robert. "We weren't diversified; we should've known better."

That wasn't the couple's only mistake. Because Robert was earning significant income, some of their decisions were driven too much by taxes, like not selling their individual holdings in the tech company that Robert worked for. They had over a million dollars in company stock that had exploded in value in the late 1990s. Because the company stock was doing so well and was a Fortune 500 company, they didn't think there was much risk. Besides, had they sold it they would have had to pay several hundred thousand dollars in taxes. Today their company stock is worth less than $90,000. Julie said, "Looking back, selling the stock and paying the taxes would have certainly been the best thing for us."

"My wife kept urging me to seek the help of a professional," said Robert. Fortunately, they finally hired an advisor who helped them to form a solid retirement plan and create a balanced and diversified portfolio. Their advisor also found ways to lower their taxes.

"Our biggest mistake was that we didn't pay enough attention to our finances," said Robert.

Julie added, "We believe we could have done the planning ourselves, but we didn't have the interest to do it ourselves."

With the help of their advisor and the plan they developed, Robert and Julie retired recently and are having the time of their lives. Their advice to others: "Unless you are willing to really study and spend an enormous amount of time on your own affairs, hire a financial advisor. That was the best financial decision we ever made."

There's no substitute for good planning. A thorough, comprehensive plan that organizes and addresses all the various elements of your retirement strategy is not only an invaluable tool for projecting needs and performance, but can ease and even decrease the anxiety and stress levels that often tum sour what's supposed to be one of the most enjoyable times in our lives. A little judicious planning early on can mean a world of difference when it comes to enjoying your retirement.

Chapter Twelve:

Finding the Right Advisor

Retirement planning is a time-consuming and complex process. Hiring a good advisor can make all the difference in the world. Advisors have the opportunity to improve their clients' quality of life and bottom line. Determining how much value an advisor can provide to their clients is largely based on their approach to financial planning and wealth management principles. Helping their clients maintain a long-term perspective and a disciplined approach is without a doubt one of the most important functions of a financial advisor.

Additional areas where an advisor can add value is by developing a written plan that includes everything that we discussed in the previous chapter, along with implementing a sound investment strategy that will incorporate their tolerance for risk while giving them the best chance to meet their long-term objectives. An advisor can also add value by having regular contact with their clients as well as providing educational classes.

If you're wondering if you should consider working with a professional, the following questions may help you decide:

1. Have I saved enough to keep me sustained without having to return to work or running out of money?

2. If I require long-term-care medical needs, how long will my money last?

3. If I retire early, should I file for Social Security at age sixty-two at a reduced amount, or should I wait until full retirement age so I can receive full benefits?

4. I can't risk losing money. Should I avoid investments that are not guaranteed, like stocks or mutual funds?

5. Am I receiving the highest possible returns with the lowest amounts of risk?

6. Am I paying too much in taxes?

7. Will my estate avoid taxes and probate, and will my assets stay out of the hands of future spouses or ex-in-laws?

8. How much can I safely withdraw from my retirement accounts? Withdraw too much and you'll run the chance of running out of money. Not withdrawing enough money can result in tax penalties or not living the lifestyle you had hoped for.

9. Can I retire early and avoid the IRS early withdraw penalty?

10. Do I have the right kind and amounts of insurances?

If you have concerns with any of the above questions, you could probably benefit by working with a good qualified planner. Financial advisors work differently than CPAs or attorneys. The mistake that some people make is working with professionals who are narrowly focused. For example, a CPA is typically looking at your taxes, and an attorney is probably just looking at your estate. A qualified financial advisor, on the other hand, plays a central role in helping you meet your life goals and achieve financial well being by considering all financial aspects of your life. An advisor should assess your current financial health by examining assets, liabilities, insurance, taxes, investments, and estate plans.

However, not all financial advisors are the same. Most people don't know how to go about hiring an advisor or what questions to ask. Spending the time to choose an advisor who is competent and trustworthy is key.

When it comes to your money, you can never be too careful. In today's fast-paced economy where the rules and opportunities change almost daily, you cannot afford to take chances. When it comes to something as important as your retirement, a good planner can be the best investment decision you'll ever make.

To help ease the anxieties you may have about hiring a planner, I've developed a few questions to ask a potential advisor. These will help you feel more on top of your retirement planning.

Ask your prospective advisor:

"How many years have you been in the business?"

You need to determine whether the advisor has enough experience. Seek help from someone who has at least five years of experience, or if not, who is a member of a team who does.

"How many clients do you have?"

You should be aware whether you are one of fifty or five hundred. If the advisor has more than fifty clients, find out what type of support staff they have. I know advisors who have hundreds of clients and may have just one support person. I don't think it's unreasonable for an advisor to have one support person for every fifty clients.

"How often do you call your clients and update their plans?"

Make sure that your expectations meet their practice. For instance, do they only call when they want to sell you something? In addition, I think that it's important to have your plan updated annually. Any plan includes assumptions and is a forecast, so it's important to update on a regular basis.

"What services do you provide your clients?"

Make sure the advisor handles what you need, whether it's comprehensive planning, estate planning, investment management, tax planning/returns, college funding, insurance, or all of the above.

"What distinguishes you from other advisors?"

The answer to this question can provide insight into the planner's strengths, priorities, and values.

"How many clients do you *lose* in a year?"
Take a hard look at any advisor who loses more than 5% of their clientele in any year, or says they never lose clients.

"How do you get paid?"
No one works for free; however, I think it's good to find out how the advisor gets paid. An advisor can be paid through commissions, fees, or a combination of both. If an advisor works strictly on commission, ask how you can be sure that the advice they give will be in your best interest. Watch out for the advisor who says that it's free or there's no cost to you!

"Do you use proprietary products?"
Proprietary products are financial products that are sold by agents or representatives who work for the same company that creates and manages the products. Of course this is a conflict of interest. An independent advisor will have a broad range of products from which to choose, and, because of this, will most likely be the best choice for you.

"What professional credentials or designations do you have, and are you registered with the SEC as an investment advisor?"
The sad truth is that anyone can hang out a shingle and call themselves a financial advisor. Education and being registered with the SEC

(RIA) is an important consideration when selecting an advisor. An RIA has a fiduciary responsibility to put their client's interest first!

Be aware that nowadays there are many designations. The following are some of the more recognized designations.

CRPC – Chartered Retirement Planning Counselor

CEA – Certified Estate Advisor

CFP – Certified Financial Planner

ChFC - Chartered Financial Consultant

CLU – Chartered Life Underwriter

APFS – Accredited Personal Financial Specialist

These designations require passing a standardized exam and typically require the planner to have continuing education to maintain their status. I'm not going to say that one is necessarily better than another; however, I do believe working with an advisor with one or more designations is your best bet. Be aware that some designations are practically worthless and only require a check to purchase one; not good!

"How do you educate your clients?"

Ask the advisor if they provide educational workshops, newsletters, websites, or anything that will help you to better understand what is going on. I believe that empowering yourself with knowledge will lead to making wiser decisions, which, of course, will increase your chances of a successful retirement.

"Do you have any client complaints, or have any disciplinary actions been taken against you or your firm?"

You should confirm this by checking the websites for FINRA (www. FINRA.org) and the SEC (www.SEC.gov). These two agencies oversee and regulate advisors. You can never know too *much about the person with whom you are possibly going to entrust your future.*

"What type of investment platform or products do you use?"
If working with an advisor is right for you, you'll want to familiarize yourself with the different investments and insurances that the advisor may use or recommend. Keep in mind that no one works for free, and no matter which method you choose, you will incur higher expenses than if you do it yourself. However, there should be added value in working with an advisor, such as time savings, better results, and increased peace of mind.

Each investment should allow the advisor to build and monitor a diversified portfolio—including equities, bonds, and cash—to meet your goals and objectives.

Next, find out if the advisor uses mutual funds or individual securities such as stocks and bonds. If the advisor is using mutual funds, find how they get compensated. They most likely are going to use either commissionable mutual funds (either "A" shares or "C" shares) or charge an advisory fee.

"A" shares pay an advisor up-front commissions, up to 5 percent. This sales charge will be deducted from your original investment. In addition, the advisor may receive an ongoing commission of a quarter of a percent. While your ongoing expenses may be a third lower than "C" shares, the advisor may not be very motivated to provide ongoing advisory services since they'll be forced to be constantly looking for new money.

"C" shares pay the planner 1% commission with an ongoing 1% commission per year, based on the size of the account. If "C" shares are used, the advisor gets paid as earned, and in theory can afford to provide ongoing advisory services, since the better you do, the better the advisor will do.

Mutual funds can be purchased either directly or in a brokerage account. I believe most advisors will prefer to use a brokerage account because it provides a consolidated statement, a multimanager approach, and allows for more convenient trading. One thing to keep in mind is ticket charges for trades. These ticket charges can range from $10 to $25. Initially this may not sound like much, but if you have a number of funds and you rebalance your portfolio four times a year, these fees can add 1% or more to your expenses.

Another option is where the advisor charges an advisory fee. An advisor may charge their client 1 to 2 percent to manage a portfolio of funds and/or individual securities. These fees can be paid directly by the client or deducted from the account. These investments will be typically held in a brokerage account. While there may be ticket charges for trades, the advisor may use funds that do not have ticket charges, which are referred to as NTC funds. If the advisor is using individual securities, there will be ticket charges; however, there won't be any fund expenses.

Under this arrangement the advisor will be compensated on an "as-earned" basis. Once again, the better you do, the better the advisor does. I feel that fee-based compensation is the best way to go because of its transparency.

Be cautious of advisors who use funds that also pay them a commission along with the fee they collect from you. Under this method the planner should be using no-load funds or funds that are purchased at NAV ("A" shares without the sales charge).

Of course, there are many more questions you can ask a prospective advisor, but at least these will give you a good start. Some other things you want to be conscious of when you're looking for an advisor include:

Integrity

Does the advisor build a plan based upon realistic assumptions? Does the advisor tell you what you *want* to hear or what you *need* to hear? Do you trust the advisor and their staff?

Competency

Is the advisor and their firm reputable? Do you know others who have had favorable experiences?

Specialization

Does the advisor specialize in retirement? Is the advisor familiar with your employer's retirement plan and procedures?

Watch Out for Wolves in Sheep's Clothing

Today there's no shortage of financial salespeople who want to be your best friend. Retirement represents a huge payday for commissioned salespeople. Many of these slick-selling commissioned salespeople sell themselves as financial planners, financial advisors, or retirement experts, but in reality they are insurance agents trying to sell you some type of annuity. These sales people are well trained and good at convincing you that the economy and stock market are near total collapse, and they have the perfect product to save the day.

Some of the most oversold products are annuities. That's not to say that there aren't good annuities that might fill a void where guarantees are needed, but I find that most annuities sold are not suitable.

The annuities of choice these days are called fixed index annuities (aka, equity index annuity and hybrid annuity). Indexed annuities are perhaps the most complicated of all annuities. This is due to a dizzying array of ways that interest can be credited, optional features, and complexities in distribution options. These types of annuities pay the largest commissions (8% to 10%) to sales agents, pay the lowest earnings, and have the most restrictive access to the policy owners' money.

The allure to these annuities is that the owner is guaranteed that they will make marketlike returns when the stock market is up, but never lose money when the market goes down. On the surface this sounds great, doesn't it? Market-linked gains with no risk! Wow, where do I sign up? Another allure is that they typically pay huge signing bonuses that are credited to the annuity.

In reality, there are limits to the upside that make these annuities no better than any traditional fixed annuity or even a bank CD; and these products often have surprises that agents don't tell you. Some of these surprises include extremely long surrender periods, often sixteen years or longer. Another little surprise is the high probability that if you buy an income guaranty and are taking withdrawals, then you will not have any money in your account by the end of the surrender period even after the bonus. This is due to low returns and high expenses.

Because these annuities pay large commissions, you'll never find a shortage of those wanting to sell you one. Many agents are skilled salespeople! Most have spent a considerable amount of time and money learning how to gain client trust with advanced sales techniques, which includes selling on fear and greed. In my opinion, most annuity advice is flawed. The costs are high, and too often I've witnessed firsthand poor advice that hurts folks more than it helps them.

Where Do You Go from Here?

We've covered a lot of material, and I certainly hope that you've found the information interesting and valuable. I believe that your best chance for a successful retirement is to empower yourself with knowledge. Retirement should be a time like no other, with traveling, golfing, fishing, or simply enjoying life. Your retirement years should not be filled with concern and anxiety.

By now you may be wondering where to go from here. Obviously, a lot of variables can affect your plans, and I've only briefly touched on the most important of them. Some may feel fairly comfortable with the information presented herein—perhaps enough even to take a crack at it themselves. If so, know that you can always consult with a financial planner if you need some guidance on specific issues.

Or perhaps you're already working with an advisor and you've read this book to supplement your knowledge. I congratulate you as well, because even though you made the decision to work with someone, it's still a good idea to educate yourself. I believe a client who is well read in the area of retirement and finance not only makes for a better client but increases his or her chances for a successful retirement. Being informed about the issues and strategies will help you to ask better questions and make informed decisions.

A wise person should know their limitations. Even if you have done a good job with accumulating retirement assets up to this point, you may find that your results could be improved by working with a planner. A planner should not only improve your investment results, but they should be helpful with other aspects of your financial life, such as when you can afford to retire, how much you can safely withdraw from your retirement accounts so that your money lasts as long as you do, how to reduce your taxes, how to decide on what insurances to have and what to get rid of, and many other issues as well.

A good planner can be your guide to a successful retirement. Since you'll be entrusting your future to this person, be sure not to take any shortcuts; and before you make your choice, interview at least three planners.

What's the biggest obstacle to achieving your picture perfect retirement? Is it taxes or inflation? Not knowing if you have the appropriate investments or allocations?

Most likely, the answer is "procrastination."

Most people put off what is most important, and that includes determining your objectives, setting priorities, and developing a strategy. Implementing and monitoring your plan requires time and commitment. Procrastination can have irreparable consequences. Unfortunately, we tend to focus on the day-today fluctuations of the stock market and the daily headlines. This type of short-term thinking almost always leads to poor decisions.

Keep your eye on the finish line. Any marathon runner or endurance athlete will tell you that the only way to win is to always, always keep the finish line in mind. You must not be distracted by unexpected changes in the weather, broken equipment, or any other obstacle that appears in your path. Similarly, successful retirees must keep their final goals in mind.

If you remember nothing else in this book, remember that, quite simply, you must plan for the future today because the future will become the present whether you plan for it or not. Here's wishing you a happy, healthy, and prosperous retirement!

Afterword

Are you ready to transform your picture-perfect retirement into reality?

An Opportunity to Take Action

Reading about retirement planning can easily give rise to nagging questions like: What does my retirement picture look like? What kind of financial shape am I in? Will I be able to afford the retirement I want? Wouldn't it be great to sit down with a pro for help? Well, here's your chance. You're invited to call our office (1-800-578-9896) to request additional information on our planning services as well as speak to one of our retirement advisors to determine if we can be of service.

In addition, we can provide you with a totally customized comprehensive retirement outlook. It is completely objective, clear, and easy to understand. It's based on your goals and objectives, not ours. We'll create a year-by-year model showing how your savings and investments will look during retirement. It will provide answers to your most important retirement questions, such as: "Am I saving enough for retirement? How long will my retirement nest egg last? Is my money invested properly? What kind of IRA is best? What role will Social Security play in my retirement? Is there any way to cut my taxes in retirement? How will inflation affect my retirement?" And one of the most popular questions: "How much can I safely withdraw from my retirement savings each year without worrying about running out of money?"

You are also invited to visit our website at www.TownsendRetirement. com to learn more about us.

We look forward to hearing from you.

Resources

Books, Magazines, Articles, and Brochures

Armond D. Budish, *Avoiding the Medicaid Trap: How to Beat the Catastrophic Costs of Nursing Home Care* (New York: Henry Holt, 1989).

Paul Light, *Baby Boomers* (New York: W.W. Norton & Co., 1988).

Lois A. Vitt and Jurg K. Siegenthaler, eds., *Encyclopedia of Financial Gerontology* (Westport, CT: Greenwood Press).

Forbes Magazine: Forbes Inc., 60 Fifth Ave., New York, NY 10011, (800) 888-9896, biweekly.

Adriane G. Berg, *Gifting to People You Love: The Complete Guide to Making Gifts, Bequests, and Investments for Children* (New York: Newmarket Press, 1996).

Harley Gordon, *How to Protect Your Life Savings from Catastrophic Illness and Nursing Homes* (Boston: Financial Strategies Press, 1994).

John Lawrence Allen, *Investor Beware: How to Protect Your Money from Wall Street's Dirty Tricks* (New York: John Wiley & Sons, 1993).

Kiplinger's Personal Finance Magazine: 1729 H Street, NW, Washington, DC 20006, (800) 544-0155, monthly.

Robert K. Ottenbourg, *Kiplinger's Retire and Thrive: Remarkable People Share Their Creative, Productive and Profitable Retirement Strategies* (Washington, DC: Kiplinger Press, 1995).

Jerry Gerber, Janet Wolff, Walter Klores, and Gene Brown, *Lifetrends* (New York: Macmillan Publishing Company).

Denis Clifford, *Make Your Own Living Trust* (Berkeley, CA: Nolo Press, 1993).

Susan Polniaszek, *Managing Your Health Care Financing*, available for a nominal charge from the United Seniors Health Cooperative, 1334 G Street, NW, 5th Floor, Washington, DC 20005, (202) 393-6222.

U.S. Department of Health and Human Services, Health Care Financing Administration, *The Medicare Handbook*, to obtain a free copy, visit your local Social Security office or call toll-free (800) 234-5755.

Charles B. Inlander and Charles K. McKay, *Medicare Made Easy* (Reading, MA: Addison-Wesley, 1988).

Money Magazine: P.O. Box 60001, Tampa, FL 33660, (800) 541-1000, monthly.

Alan Pifer and Lydia Bronte, eds., *Our Aging Society: Paradox and Promise* (New York: W.W. Norton & Co.).

Denis Clifford, *Plan Your Estate* (Berkeley, CA: Nolo Press, 1992).

Denis Clifford, *Simple Will Book: How to Prepare a Legally Valid Will*, 2nd ed. (Berkeley, CA: Nolo Press, 1995).

Joseph L. Matthews, *Social Security, Medicare and Pensions*, 6th ed. (Berkeley, CA: Nolo Press, 1996).

Arsen J. Darnay, ed., *Statistical Record of Older Americans* (Detroit: Gale Research Inc.).

Twila Slesnick and John C. Suttle, *Taking Your Money Out: IRAs, 401(k)s and Other Retirement Plans* (Berkeley, CA: Nolo Press), not exactly light reading, but an excellent starting point.

William C. Cockerham, *This Aging Society* (Upper Saddle River, NJ: Prentice Hall).

Tomorrow's Choices: Preparing Now for Future Legal, Financial, and Health Care Decisions (D13479), and *Health Care Powers of Attorney* (D 13895): AARP Fulfillment, 601 E. Street, NW, Washington, DC 20049; (800) 424-3410.

United Seniors Health Cooperative, *Long Term Care: A Dollar and Sense Guide* Washington, DC, 1994, 1331 H Street, NW, Washington, DC 20005; (202) 393-6222.

Pension Benefit Guarantee Corp., *Your Pension: Things You Should Know About Your Pension Plan* (brochure), 2020 K Street, NW, Washington, DC 20006.

Websites

www.brill.com. Interactive mutual fund information.

www.irs.gov/prod/cover.html .Internal Revenue Service.

www.insure.com. Insurance News Network.

www.irajunction.com. A fledgling site offered by mPower, which also runs another top investor website called 401kafe.com.

www.irahelp.com. Sponsored by CPA and IRA newsletter publisher Ed Slott, the chief attraction is a forum where he'll help answer your IRA questions.

www.investools.com. Independent investment and financial information.

www.mfmag.com. Mutual funds information from *Mutual Funds Magazine*.

www.ssa.gov. Social Security online.

www.firstclassretirement.com. My own firm's website.

Associations and Organizations

Health Insurance Association of America, 1001 Pennsylvania Avenue, NW Washington, DC. 20004-2599, (800) 942-4242.

Medicaid (Medi-Cal in California)—For more information about eligibility and benefits, contact the state department that administers Medicaid, sometimes called the Department of Public Social Services, Department of Human Services, Department of Welfare, or Department of Health. Check the government section of your telephone book.

National Association of Insurance Commissioners, 120 West 12th Street, Suite 1100, Kansas City, MO 64105; (816) 842-3600.

National Council on Aging, 409 3rd Street, SW, Suite 200, Washington, DC 20024; (202) 479-1200.

Social Security Administration—Visit a local office for information about Medicare or call toll-free: (800) 234-5755.

State Department of Insurance—Check the government section of your phone book for the address and telephone number.

SEC (Securities and Exchange Commission) Office of Consumer Affairs, 450 Fifth Street, NW, Room 2111, Mail Stop 2-6, Washington, DC 20549; (202) 272-7440; (202) 272-7065 (telecommunications for the deaf); free brochures.

Bibliography

Books

Dychtwald, Ken. *Age Power.* New York: Jeremey P. Tarcher, 2000.

Principles of Retirement Planning, 4th Edition. Chicago: Dearborn Financial Publishing, 2001.

Townsend, Jeff. *The Master Plan.* Denver: The Publishing Cooperative, 2001.

Articles

Barlett, Donald L., and James B. Steele, "The Great Retirement Ripoff," *Time* magazine, 31 October 2005.

Editorial, "A False Start on Social Security," *New York Times*, 3 December 2004.

Editorial, "For the Record on Social Security," *New York Times*, 10 January 2005.

Editorial, "A Bridge to Sell, *New York Times*, 24 January 2005.

Editorial, "A Spoonful of Sugar," *New York Times*, 1 February 2005.

Kasich, John, "A New Index for Social Security," *New York Times*, 1 December 2004.

Krugman, Paul, "Inventing a Crisis," *New York Times*, 7 December 2004.

Krugman, Paul, "The Iceberg Cometh," *New York Times*, 11 January 2005.

Krugman, Paul, "That Magic Moment," *New York Times*, 18 January 2005.

Krugman, Paul, "Many Unhappy Returns," *New York Times*, 1 February 2005.

Lowenstein, Roger, "A Question of Numbers," *New York Times Magazine*, 16 January 2005

Pear, Robert, "Social Security Agency Is Enlisted to Push Its Own Revision," *New York Times*, 16 January 2005.

Rosenbaum, David E. and Robin Toner, "Introducing Private Investments to the Safety Net," *New York Times*, 3 February 2005.

Schwartz, Barry, "Choose and Lose," *New York Times*, 5 January 2005.

Bibliography

"Secure Your Future Through Retirement Planning," *Fortune Magazine,* 23 November 1998.

Sperling, Gene, "No Pain, No Savings," *New York Times,* 5 January 2005.

Stevenson, Richard W., "Bush's Social Security Plan Is Said to Require Vast Borrowing," *New York Times,* 28 November 2004.

Stevenson, Richard W., "Social Security Proposals Split Republicans," *New York Times,* 6 January 2005.

Survey, *USA Today,* 12 March 1996.

Walsh, Mary Williams, "Taking the Wheel Before a Pension Runs Into Trouble," *New York Times,* 30 January 2005.

"20 Crucial IRA Tips," *Mutual Funds* magazine, February 2000.

"70 Years of Social Security," *Denver Post,* 14 August 2005.

Websites

http://www.ahrq.gov/consumer/insuranc .htm#head 1

Made in the
USA
Middletown, DE